THE KEYS ARE BEING PASSED:
Race, Law, Religion and The
Legacy of the Civil Rights Movement

By

Jonathan C. Augustine

www.jayaugustine.com

Houston, Texas

Jonathan C. Augustine

ROM Books
ROM Publishing, LLC
P.O. Box 2047
Houston, Texas 77252

ROM Digital Ink Press®
is a registered trademark of ROM Publishing, LLC

Published by arrangement with the author

Printing History
First Edition April 2014
Second Edition May 2014

Library of Congress Control Number: 2014937296

ISBN: 0-615-99577-2

www.ROMPublishing.com

This book is lovingly dedicated to my daughter, Jillian Claire Augustine. Born in 2004, Jillian became part of a world that was vastly different from the one into which I was born thirty-three years earlier. Moreover, the world in which Jillian is now growing up is even more different than it was during the revolutionary time commonly known as the American Civil Rights Movement.

This book explores the connection between law and religion that made the Movement more than just a fruitless utopian ideal. Rigorous research I conducted during my years as a practicing lawyer and seminary student inspired me to share my thoughts with you in this book. It is my sincere hope that it will inspire Jillian's generation, just as the actions of the courageous participants of the actual Movement have inspired mine.

I originally wrote some portions of this book for publication in various law journals. I owe a deep debt of gratitude to the respective editorial staffs of those law journals that I had the pleasure of working with to communicate my ideas. In addition to the particular individuals acknowledged in the original scholarly works, I want to especially thank the *Southern California Interdisciplinary Law Journal*, the *University of San Francisco Law Review*, *Louisiana Law Review*, *University of Louisville Law Review*, and the *Loyola Law Review*.

Jonathan C. Augustine
Baton Rouge, Louisiana
March 20, 2014

Foreword

I was blessed to attend Spellman College in Atlanta, Georgia, from 1960 to 1964. Both during and after my college years, I witnessed monumental events like the Freedom Rides (1961), March on Washington (1963), as well as passage of the Civil Rights Act (1964) and the Voting Rights Act (1965). In connection with my unwavering faith in God, these events had a major influence on my life. I decided to become a lawyer and was blessed to be one of the first African-American women to graduate from the Louisiana State University Law School in 1969. You might say that I was prepared to accept "the keys" of social responsibility and legacy associated with being a person of faith who lived during the American Civil Rights Movement.

In the sixteenth chapter of the *Gospel of Matthew*, immediately before predicting the necessity of his suffering and death, Jesus is described as passing "the keys" on to his disciple, Peter, and calling Peter the rock upon which he will build the church. Peter did not seek out the legacy and responsibility Jesus was preparing to pass on to him. Instead, because of his faith, Peter found himself in the position of having no choice but to accept the keys.

In 2014, exactly fifty-years after I graduated from college, the United States of America is in the midst of several years of celebration, honoring the leadership and courage of so many people that made the Civil Rights Movement possible. In the heart of that on-going celebration, I find myself as the first African-American Chief Justice of the Louisiana Supreme Court. While some might correctly say that I am a beneficiary of the courageous acts of so many that paved the way for me, I also recognize that sociopolitical circumstances allowed me to accept "the keys" that were mine to receive.

In *The Keys Are Being Passed*, the author, an accomplished attorney, pastor, and I'm proud to share, my former law clerk, honors and celebrates the 50th

Anniversary of the Civil Rights Movement by bringing together the disciplines of law and religion and challenging its readers, especially those who have faith in God, to become engaged in social affairs affecting their communities by accepting the keys of responsibility and legacy. This book honors the theological motivation behind the many men and women who literally risked their lives in selflessly pursuing the greater communal good of justice and equality for all by participating in, for example, the Freedom Rides, segregated lunch counter sit-ins, and the Bloody Sunday march for voting rights over Selma, Alabama's Edmund Pettis Bridge. The book also examines how so many elected officials, including myself, benefit from the interfaith movement that led to passage of the Voting Rights Act and how President Johnson's Great Society initiative led to passage of the Elementary and Secondary Education Act of 1965, one of the least talked about but most important laws ever passed by Congress.

In addition to detailing the political and socioeconomic impact of several legislative enactments and civil rights victories won in the judicial system, *The Keys Are Being Passed* also describes the Civil Rights Movement as a precursor to the Environmental Justice Movement that directly affects so many minority communities. Further, the book notes the historical and moral significance of environmental justice by tracing its origins back to Judeo-Christian biblical texts found in the *Book of Genesis* and the *Book of Revelation*. The book's interdisciplinary approach honors and celebrates the Golden Anniversary of the movement I remember so well in a unique and refreshing way.

Finally, written by a seminary-trained pastor and former civil rights lawyer, *The Keys Are Being Passed* also details "the social gospel" in the transcripts of some previously shared sermons. They describe the sociopolitical importance of today's church—the church that Jesus built on the faith of his disciple Peter—by explaining the two planes of Jesus' cross. The sermons discuss the interconnectedness of the Christian cross' vertical plane, dealing with the individual's salvation and relationship with the divine, while also discussing its horizontal plane, describing the church's moral and social responsibility to help the most marginalized in society. Indeed, while Christians believe Jesus died for individual salvation (the vertical plane), the sermons also stress that Jesus lived for social service (the horizontal plane), helping the poor, sick, and marginalized—those that most needed assistance.

The Keys Are Being Passed is a timely work of historical and contemporary importance. It honors the 50th Anniversary of the Civil Rights Movement by emphasizing the importance of today's generation accepting the keys of legacy and responsibility from those that changed the world when I was college student. We all must accept our respective keys, just as Peter accepted his keys from Jesus.

> Hon. Bernette Joshua Johnson
> Chief Justice, Supreme Court of Louisiana
> New Orleans, Louisiana
> March 11, 2014

Author's Note

Now when Jesus came into the district of Caesarea Philippi, he asked his disciples, "Who do people say that the Son of Man is?" And they said, "Some say John the Baptist, but others Elisha, and still others Jeremiah or one of the prophets." He said to them, "But who do you say that I am?" Simon Peter answered, "You are the Messiah, the Son of the living God." And Jesus answered him, "Blessed are you Simon, son of Jonah! For flesh and blood has not revealed this to you, but my Father in heaven. *And I tell you, you are Peter, and on this rock, I will build my church*, and the gates of Hades will not prevail against it. *I will give you the keys of the kingdom of heaven, and whatever you bind on earth, will be bound in heaven, and whatever you loose on earth shall be loosed in heaven.*"

- *Matthew* 16:13-19 (NRSV) (emphasis added)

"[T]he Christian gospel is a two-way road. On the one hand, it seeks to change the souls of men, and thereby unite them with God; on the other hand, it seeks to change the environmental conditions of men so that the soul will have a chance after it is changed. Any religion that professes to be concerned with the souls of men and is not concerned with the slums that damn them, the economic conditions that strangle them, and the social conditions that cripple them is a dry-as-dust religion."

- Martin Luther King, Jr., *Stride Toward Freedom*

The writer of the *Gospel of Matthew* records Jesus as recognizing Peter's faith and giving Peter "the keys" to the kingdom. According to Christian theology, Jesus led a sect of Judaism that became the Christian church. By symbolically giving Peter the keys to the church, Jesus gave Peter responsibility, along with a legacy that included advocating equality for and acceptance of all people, particularly those marginalized by society.

Courageous and forward thinking members of the Christian church fueled the Civil Rights Movement. Ministers worked across ecumenical lines with committed students and laypersons, and with some members and clergy of other faiths, such as Judaism, to make manifest in America the ideas of equality once advocated and practiced by Jesus. Further, because Christian theology regards Jesus' suffering and crucifixion as redemptive, the Movement's leaders made and encouraged personal and physical sacrificial suffering for the greater communal good. Indeed, this theological framework was the proverbial glue that bound most aspects of the Movement together. This Christian-influenced thinking manifested in the freedom rides, lunch counter sit-ins, and countless marches, including the infamous Bloody Sunday march for voting rights in Alabama. Indeed, the Movement's leaders juxtaposed law and religion to literally change America.

The proverbial keys of the movement are responsibility and legacy, just as are the proverbial keys Jesus gave Peter. As we celebrate the fiftieth anniversary of the Movement's legacy, its surviving leaders are passing those same keys to a new generation that must accept their responsibility. Although this generation's leaders have different battles than those fought fifty years ago, much like Peter, the keys are theirs to accept.

Part One of this book, "The Theology of Civil Disobedience," includes four chapters. The first three focus on the Movement's theological underpinnings, its development of the First Amendment, and the fruits of the Movement's battles: primarily, passage of the Voting

Rights Act of 1965. Its fourth chapter is the transcript of a sermon, "The Keys Are Being Passed," that I shared with the congregation of New Orleans' St. Paul African Methodist Episcopal Church for a Martin Luther King, Jr. holiday celebration, drawing on the spiritual and temporal connection between the keys of legacy and responsibility, then and now.

Part Two, "Law Religion and Environmental Justice," contains three chapters, building upon the foundation established in Part One. Part Two transitions by examining the ongoing environmental justice movement, an outgrowth of the original Movement that was specifically led by a social justice-oriented clergy and environmental activist communities in the South. In addition to exploring the concept of environmental justice today, Part Two looks at the environmental justice movement in the afterlife by specifically exploring the concept of environmental justice from the Holy Bible's *Book of Revelation*. It concludes with a sermon on empowerment, "You Have Power," that I shared at Dillard University's Lawless Memorial Chapel.

Finally, Part Three of this book, "Leveling the Playing Field," contains two chapters focused on the great equalizer, education reform, arguably the greatest of the Movement's accomplishments. While the fight for equality in public education was originally led by Thurgood Marshall and the advocates that won *Brown v. Board of Education* (1954), the fight for education reform was truly launched with Congress' passage of the Elementary and Secondary Education Act of 1965, the statutory precursor to the controversial and much talked about No Child Left Behind Act of 2001. Part Three concludes with a final sermon, "The Impatient Act of Waiting," shared as part of Greater Mount Carmel Baptist Church's Rededication Sunday. It directly addresses the challenges we all face today in accepting the keys to our own legacy, while celebrating the fiftieth anniversary of the Movement.

TABLE OF CONTENTS

PART ONE
The Theology of Civil Disobedience

Chapter 1   "Martin Luther King, Jr. and the Suffering Servant: The Theology of the Civil Rights Movement".. 2

Charter 2   "Civil Disobedience and Civil Challenge: Where Law and Religion Meet the First Amendment"... 21

Charter 3   "The Fruits of Civil Disobedience: Passage of the Voting Rights Act of 1965 and Its Impact on the Movement"............. 33

Chapter 4   "The Keys Are Being Passed".................... 51

PART TWO
Law, Religion and Environmental Justice

Chapter 5   "The Origins of Environmental Justice: The Holy Bible ....……...... 63

Chapter 6   "Environmental Justice and *Letter From Birmingham Jail*" 75

Chapter 7   "You Have Power"................................... 89

PART THREE
Leveling the Playing Field: the Ongoing Fight for Education Reform

Chapter 8   "Education reform as Part of the Civil Rights Movement: The Interest Convergence 2.0"............................. 100

Chapter 9   "Leaving no Child Behind Means
                Establishing Equality in Public
                Education".. 109

Chapter 10   "The Impatient Act of Waiting"...... 131

PART ONE

The Theology of Civil Disobedience

Chapter 1

Martin Luther King, Jr. and the Suffering Servant:
The Theology of the Civil Rights Movement

> *[T]he movement's bold strand*
> *of nonviolence (and we will*
> *surely teach that there were*
> *other, sometimes competing,*
> *strands) provides a chance and*
> *a challenge that cannot be left*
> *unmet. It allows us to go with*
> *our students as deeply as we*
> *choose toward the sources of*
> *that lifestyle, delving, for*
> *instance, into the experience*
> *and experiments of Gandhi*
> *and his movement, into the*
> *paths of the Buddha, working*
> *our way toward Jesus of*
> *Nazareth and his justice-*
> *obsessed brother and sister*
> *prophets of Israel, moving*
> *quietly, firmly into the river-*
> *deep meditations of Howard*
> *Thurman- perhaps even*
> *reading more of King than the*
> *worthy and well-worn 1963*
> *March on Washington "I Have*
> *a Dream" speech. We must*
> *work our way into the depths*
> *of spirit which supplied the*
> *movement with so much of its*
> *early power.*

-Vincent Harding, *Hope and History*[1]

In recent years, the term "civil disobedience" has resurged in popular American usage for at least two reasons. There have been manifestations of discontent such as the recent "occupy movement," a social resistance effort in response to social and economic inequalities (*e.g.*, Occupy Wall Street) that seeks to bring attention to inequities by literally occupying certain areas, usually in contravention to publicized warnings. Closer to home, however, in observing the fiftieth anniversary of several milestone events in the American Civil Rights Movement (the Movement), Americans are reminded how popular civil disobedience was in American culture.

The Theological Underpinnings of the Movement

Although the Movement's impetus came from outside of the church, the clergy accepted leadership in a newly developing "social gospel" and provided Black Americans with a sense of stability in the midst of ongoing social change. Black members of the clergy were natural leaders of the Movement because of their independence. Like Black lawyers who served a primarily Black clientele, African American pastors who served predominately Black congregations were largely immune from white reprisal. The theologically based interfaith organization that provided a cooperative infrastructure for the clergy's active involvement in the Movement was the Southern Christian Leadership Conference ("SCLC"), founded in 1957.[2] Through the Black church, ministers helped facilitate the Movement by organizing and leading bus boycotts across the South.[3] In addition, Fred Shuttlesworth, an Alabama clergyman, was instrumental in organizing an alternative civil rights group in Birmingham after the state legislature outlawed the National Association for the Advancement of Colored People ("NAACP").[4]

The primary theological principles that motivated the Movement were: (1) the concept of evangelical liberalism, which envisioned an active role for Christians and the

3

church in reforming social institutions; (2) the moral duty to disobey unjust laws—a duty that flowed from evangelical liberalism; (3) Martin Luther King, Jr.'s emphasis on love and equality; and (4) the messianic suffering servant theology. This section explores the manner in which these theological principles permeated and motivated both the Movement's clergy leadership and lay participants. Because of his influential role and leadership, King and his contributions receive special attention in this book.

Evangelical Liberalism

The Movement's foundational theology, led by the SCLC and many ordained clergy, was based on the concept of evangelical liberalism. Evangelical liberalism focused on human goodness and the church's necessary social role in society at large.[5] In contrast, unlike the evangelical conservatism as practiced in the 1950s, which envisioned a strict separation between the church and social and political issues, evangelical liberalism envisioned Christians and the church playing an active role in reforming or eradicating unjust social and political institutions—like slavery and segregation—to reflect Christian ideals.[6] In a sense, evangelical liberalism was more present-minded than evangelical conservatism in that it attempted to focus Christians on society's existing injustices, rather than exclusively on the future rewards of an afterlife.[7] In other words, King and the Black church's "social gospel" were called upon to deal with the issues in the kingdom at hand, not just the concept of salvation in the kingdom to come.

Disobedience of Unjust Laws

The Movement was characterized by a belief that people had a moral duty to deliberately disobey unjust laws. With respect to King's theological beliefs regarding

4

this duty, Peter Paris, professor emeritus at Princeton Theological Seminary, explains that "[s]ince King had advocated time and again that those who acquiesce to evil participate in promoting evil and are, therefore, as much the agents of evil as the initiators themselves, he concluded that *one could not be moral by obeying immoral laws*."[8]

Any decision by the leaders and participants in the Movement to engage in civil disobedience was the product of a deliberate process. Thus, before acting, they had to determine whether a law was "just" or "unjust." In this regard, King was influenced by St. Augustine, as reflected in King's writing the following in his famed *Letter from a Birmingham Jail*:

> You express a great deal of anxiety over our willingness to break unjust laws. This is certainly a legitimate concern. Since we so diligently urge people to obey the Supreme Court's decision of 1954 outlawing segregation in the public schools, at first glance it may seem rather paradoxical for us consciously to break laws. One may well ask: "How can you advocate breaking some laws and obeying others?" The answer lies in the fact that there are two types of laws: just and unjust...One has not only a legal but a moral responsibility to obey just laws. Conversely, one has a moral responsibility to disobey unjust laws. I would agree

5

> with St. Augustine that "an
> unjust law is no law at all."[9]

King's explanation to his fellow members of the clergy regarding the Movement's civil disobedience in Birmingham did not stop with his reliance on St. Augustine. King went further to expound on his discernment between "just" and "unjust" laws to support his actions. For example, he continued by asking:

> Now, what is the difference
> between the two? How does
> one determine whether a law
> is just or unjust? A just law is
> a man-man code that squares
> with the moral law or the law
> of God. An unjust law is a law
> that is out of harmony with
> the moral law. To put it in the
> terms of St. Thomas Aquinas:
> an unjust law is a human law
> not rooted in eternal law and
> natural law. Any law that
> uplifts human personality is
> just. Any law that degrades
> human personality is unjust.
> All segregation statutes are
> unjust because segregation
> distorts the soul and damages
> the personality. It gives the
> segregator a false sense of
> superiority and the segregated
> a false sense of inferiority.[10]

After making the requisite determination, the Movement's leaders decided whether they would follow or peacefully disobey the law. If they deemed a law unjust, they deliberately engaged in active disobedience. For example, although there is a popular misconception that Rosa Parks' historic act of civil disobedience that precipitated the Montgomery Bus Boycott was merely that of a fatigued worker, scholars observe that her action was actually a deliberate and conscientious objection. As, Adam Fairclough explained in his book *To Redeem the Soul of America: The Southern Leadership Conference and Martin Luther King, Jr.:*

> Her decision to choose arrest rather than humiliation when driver J. F. Blake ordered her to give up her seat on December 1, 1955, was more than the impulsive gesture of a seamstress with sore feet. Although shy and unassuming, Rosa Parks held strong and well-developed views about the inequities of segregation. Long active in the NAACP, she had served as secretary of the local branch. In the summer of 1953 she spent two weeks at Highlander Folk School in Monteagle, Tennessee, an institution which assiduously encouraged interracial amity. Founded and run by Myles Horton, Highlander flouted the local segregation laws and gave black and white Southerners a virtually unique opportunity to meet and mingle on equal terms. Rosa Parks' protest on the Cleveland Avenue bus was the purposeful act of a politically aware person.[11]

7

King's belief in a moral duty to disobey unjust laws was tempered with a respect for the rule of law, as he and his followers accepted the penalties for violating laws they considered unjust. Indeed, King contended that the breaking of unjust laws must be done in the spirit of love and with a willingness to accept the penalty, such that the latter attitude demonstrates a high regard for law in principle. Moreover, highly reputed church historians view the Movement's theological underpinning as a faithful willingness to suffer the consequences of direct actions, such as sit-ins and marches, for the anticipated reform of an unjust system.[12]

Love and Equality

King's socio-political theology was, first and foremost, undergirded by a Christian philosophy of love.[13] As Professor Paris writes, King believed:

> Not only was love in the form of nonviolent resistance in accord with God's will, but, he claimed, it was the most effective means available to the oppressed in their fight against injustice. Indeed, he contended that there would be no permanent solution to the race problem until oppressed people developed the capacity to love their enemies.[14]

The way King manifested his belief in a socio-political theological basis for civil disobedience also shows the level of detail he applied to his approach to seeking justice. He appeared to prefer civil disobedience to court challenges of unjust laws. It is likely that his unfavorable experiences in the courts led to his increased adoption of means to take extra-judicial actions. For example, when King and others in the Movement took court action to challenge Birmingham Commissioner Eugene "Bull" Connor's discriminatory refusal to issue a parade permit that would have allowed clergy members to peacefully and legally assemble on Good Friday in 1963, they lost before the Supreme Court.[15] After an Alabama court enjoined the ministers from assembling, the Supreme Court agreed, looking solely at the fact that the protestors lacked a permit.[16] The Court neglected to acknowledge the discriminatory motives behind Connor's denial of the permit, when it wrote in its opinion supporting Connor's action:

> The rule of law that Alabama followed in this case reflects a belief that in the fair administration of justice no man can be judge in his own case, however exalted his station, however righteous his motives, and irrespective of his race, color, politics, or religion. This Court cannot hold that the petitioners were constitutionally free to ignore all the procedures of the law and carry their battle to the streets. One may sympathize with the petitioners' impatient commitment to their cause. But respect for judicial process is a small price to pay for the civilizing hand of law, which alone can give abiding meaning to constitutional freedom.[17]

Jonathan C. Augustine

Despite this legal defeat, King remained steadfast in
his theological convictions that the Movement—essentially
an interdisciplinary juxtaposition of law and religion—
placed his actions on a moral high ground that preempted
state law. As a testament to his theology, on December 5,
1955, at the onset of the Montgomery Bus Boycott, King
shared the following affirmation of civil disobedience while
speaking in Montgomery:

> [W]e are not wrong in what we
> are doing. If we are wrong,
> then the Supreme Court of
> this nation is wrong. If we are
> wrong, the Constitution of the
> United States is wrong. If we
> are wrong, God Almighty is
> wrong. If we are wrong, Jesus
> of Nazareth was merely a
> utopian dreamer and never
> came down to earth. If we are
> wrong, justice is a lie. And we
> are determined here in
> Montgomery to work and fight
> until justice runs down like
> water, and righteousness like
> a mighty stream.[18]

From King's theological perspective, therefore, human
equality stemmed from the identity of all humans as being
children of God.[19] Indeed, this is the very essence of the
communal love of humankind known as agape. As
Professor Paris observed:

> King's vision of the kinship of
> humans as a direct corollary of
> the parenthood of God
> pervaded his entire thought.

Only the divine principal of
love can hold the diversity of
humankind together in a
harmonious community. That
kindredness of persons under
the parenthood of God was, in
King's mind, the kingdom of
God...His fundamental ethical
norm was the Christian
understanding of love as
presented primarily in the
Sermon on the Mount and as
symbolized most vividly in the
cross on which Jesus died
while forgiving his enemies.
King viewed Jesus as the
supreme manifestation of that
religious and ethical
principle.[20]

It is also apparent that in keeping with the
Movement's theology of equality, clergy and lay persons
alike engaged in direct action, just as Rosa Parks did when
she refused to give up her bus seat in the act of civil
disobedience that served as the Movement's genesis. King
actually suggested that direct action was systematically
designed to create crisis as a prelude to peace. In any
nonviolent campaign, there are four basic steps: (1)
collection of the facts to determine whether injustices exist,
(2) negotiation, (3) self-purification, and (4) direct action.[21]
King explained:

We had no alternative except to
prepare for direct action, whereby
we would present our very bodies
as a means of laying our case
before the conscience of the local
and national community. You may

11

well ask: "Why direct action? Why sit-ins, marches and so forth? Isn't negotiation a better path?" Indeed, this is the very purpose of direct action. Nonviolent direct action seeks to create such a crisis that a community which has constantly refused to negotiate is forced to confront the issue. It seeks so to dramatize the issue that it can no longer be ignored. My citing the creation of tension as part of the work of the nonviolent-resister may sound rather shocking. But I must confess that I am not afraid of the word "tension." I have earnestly opposed violent tension, but there is a type of constructive, nonviolent tension which is necessary for growth. Just as Socrates felt that it was necessary to create a tension in the mind so that individuals could rise from the bondage of myths and half-truths to the unfettered realm of creative analysis and objective appraisal, so must we see the need for nonviolent gadflies to create the kind of tension in society that will help men rise from the dark depths of prejudice and racism to the majestic heights of understanding and brotherhood. The purpose of our direct-action program is to create a situation so crisis-packed that it will inevitably open the door to negotiation.[22]

The Messianic Suffering Servant and the Movement

Part of the theology of civil disobedience in the Movement can be traced to the Old Testament's scriptures which foretold of the coming of the messiah that would suffer on behalf of Israel and restore them to the Kingdom of God, in concert with the New Testament theology that Jesus' suffering redeemed those he loved and reconciled them in relationship with the divine. As an ordained Christian minister, King believed Jesus' cross symbolized suffering and victory, and that Jesus suffered such a brutal death because he consistently lived a life of love. He once stated:

> In [Jesus' crucifixion], history witnesses the sacrificial element implied by love. Love is no guarantor against persecution and suffering. In confronting evil it risks the possibility of suffering and death...And so, Christ died praying for his executioners, thereby manifesting the community his life and mission exemplified. Although he was crucified, love had not been destroyed, even in its darkest hour. And that is the victory the cross symbolizes. Those who love may suffer at the hands of injustice, but injustice cannot destroy the love of God, which is always redemptive.[23]

Accordingly, the very center of King's theology—and arguably the theology of the Movement—was a belief that

13

God's love was redemptive,[24] especially through unmerited suffering. From a Christological perspective, therefore, the suffering servant theology manifested in the life and death of Jesus the prophet from Galilee. King's perspective on this aspect of Christology is evident in the following excerpt from an article he wrote in the February 6, 1957, issue of *Christian Century*:

> *There is something at the very center of our faith which reminds us that Good Friday may reign for a day, but ultimately it must give way to the triumphant beat of the Easter drums.* Evil may so shape events that Caesar will occupy a palace and Christ a cross, but one day that same Christ will rise up and split history into A.D. and B.C., so that even the life of Caesar must be dated by his name. So in Montgomery we can walk and never get weary, because we know that there will be a great camp meeting in the promised land of freedom and justice.[25]

Further, King derived his Judeo-Christian perspective on redemptive suffering from messianic scriptures. For example, *Isaiah*'s Fourth Servant Song, presumably written to provide hope and inspiration to the children of Israel while suffering during the Babylonian Exile, depicts extreme and unmerited suffering in the name of redemption.[26] The Fourth Servant Song provides the following:

Surely he has borne our infirmities and carried our diseases; yet we accounted him stricken, struck down by God, and afflicted. But he was wounded for our transgressions, crushed for our iniquities; upon him was the punishment that made us whole, and by his bruises we are healed...He was oppressed, and he was afflicted, yet he did not open his mouth...For he was cut off from the land of the living, stricken for the transgression of my people. They made his grave with the wicked and his tomb with the rich, although he had done no violence, and there was no deceit in his mouth...Out of his anguish he shall see light; he shall find satisfaction through his knowledge. The righteous one, my servant, shall make many righteous, and he shall bear their inequities. Therefore I will allot him a portion with the great, and he shall divide the spoil with the strong; because he poured out himself to death, and was numbered with the transgressors; yet he bore the sin of many, and made intercession for the transgressors.[27]

Scholars debate whether the redemptive suffering was done by the people of Israel or whether it was messianic in describing Jesus, the foretold Christ who would suffer on behalf of all people.[28] Regardless, in the Movement's context, this suffering servant theology was epitomized by the willingness of many students, clergy, and lay activists to endure beatings, be spat upon, and be the targets of trained attack dogs and water hoses, all because they believed their temporal suffering was for a greater and sustaining cause.

Just as King's theology viewed his personal suffering as redemptive, he viewed the sacrifices of others engaged in the Movement as redemptive, too.[29] This is what the theology of civil disobedience was all about. In May of 1961, for example, the Congress for Racial Equality, a multiracial group of direct action activists that was originally founded in 1942, challenged the Deep South's segregationist interstate commerce practices by sending buses of college students and other young activists on "Freedom Rides" from Washington, DC, to New Orleans. In Alabama and Mississippi, racist mobs violently attacked and beat the Freedom Riders, as they were known. By embracing a theological perspective of the suffering servant enduring for a greater good, the Freedom Riders significantly affected the Movement's momentum leading up to the passage of the Voting Rights Act of 1965 by placing their personal safety and security behind the greater causes in which they believed.

Professor Raymond Arsenault writes about the Freedom Riders' suffering servant mentality in describing their willingness to literally sacrifice their bodies in their nonviolent protests against racial segregation in interstate commerce:

> Deliberately provoking a crisis of authority, the Riders challenged federal officials to enforce the law and uphold the

constitutional right to travel without being subjected to degrading and humiliating racial restrictions. *Most amazingly, they did so knowing that their actions would almost certainly provoke a savage and violent response from militant white supremacists. Invoking the philosophy of nonviolent direct action, they willingly put their bodies on the line for the cause of racial justice.*[30]

King also recognized the Freedom Riders' unwavering commitment to endure suffering in order to achieve justice on November 16, 1961, speaking before the annual meeting of the Fellowship for the Concerned, a multiracial fellowship group affiliated with the Southern Regional Council. He stated:

I can remember the times that we've been together, I remember that night in Montgomery, Alabama, when we had stayed up all night discussing the Freedom Rides, and that morning came to see that it was necessary to go on with the Freedom Rides, that we would not in all good conscience call an end to the Freedom Rides at that point. *And I remember the first group got ready to leave, to take a bus for Jackson, Mississippi, we all joined hands and started singing together. "We shall overcome, we shall overcome." And something within me said, now how is it that these students can sing this, they are going down to Mississippi, they are going to face hostile and jeering mobs, and yet they could sing, "We shall overcome." They may even face physical death, and yet they could sing, "We shall overcome." Most of them realized that they would be thrown into jail, and yet they could sing, "We shall overcome, we are not afraid."* Then something caused me to see at that moment the real meaning of the movement. That students had faith in the future. That the movement was based on hope, that this movement had something within it that says somehow even though the arc of the moral universe is long, it bends toward justice...*Before the victory is won some may have to get scarred up, but we shall overcome. Before the victory of brotherhood is achieved, some will maybe face physical death, but we shall overcome. Before the victory is won, some will lose jobs, some will be called communists, and reds, merely because they*

> *believe in brotherhood, some*
> *will be dismissed as dangerous*
> *rabblerousers and agitators*
> *merely because they're*
> *standing up for what is right,*
> *but we shall overcome.*[31]

From a theological perspective, therefore, the Freedom Riders shared King's redemptive suffering sentiment as they achieved victories for freedom of speech and association in interstate commerce.[32]

Indeed, the same willingness to endure unmerited brutality for the accomplishment of larger and more far-reaching goals motivated the Bloody Sunday marchers in their attempts to bring attention to the need for voting rights legislation in 1965. On the morning of March 7, 1965, more than 500 demonstrators, including ordained clergy, members of the SCLC and the Student Nonviolent Coordinating Committee assembled at Morris Brown African Methodist Episcopal Church in Selma.[33] Those assembled planned a peaceful demonstration in support of the unbiased right to vote, along with a voter registration drive.[34] The end result, however, was that uniformed officers brutally attacked the peaceful demonstrators. The willingness of both the Freedom Riders and the Bloody Sunday marchers to endure suffering to garner rights gained the attention of the nation and ultimately facilitated legal advances in their favor.

There is an old cliché that provides "The more things change, the more they stay the same." Many of the leaders of the Movement are gone. Although the historical Movement was fifty years ago, many social injustices and inequities still fuel social resistance. Indeed, although the battles may be different, the popular response to social inequality and injustice remains the same, as exemplified by many post-modern activists.

Just as Jesus passed the keys of church—the keys of legacy and responsibility—to Peter, King and the

Jonathan C. Augustine

Movement's other leaders are also passing those keys on to the current generation of leaders. Peter did not have a choice to say no and decline acceptance of the keys and neither do society's current leaders. The church, acting through both clergy and lay persons, must remain actively engaged in fighting social injustices today in the post-modern era, just as it was engaged in the same during the Movement. The keys are being passed and this generation must accept them.

Chapter 2

Civil Disobedience and Civil Challenge: Where Law and Religion Meet the First Amendment

> *Congress shall make no law...abridging the freedom of speech, or of the press..." But those fourteen words cannot in themselves account for our great freedom...[S]omething has happened to the fourteen words of the speech and press clauses. Their meaning has changed. Or, more accurately, the understanding of those words has changed judges' understanding and the public's.*

- Anthony Lewis, *Freedom for the Thought That We Hate*[35]

> *"To call for disobedience to the law is acceptable behavior when such law transgresses upon the city of God."*

- William F. Buckley, Jr.[36]

The Movement's reform-oriented agenda essentially moved on parallel tracks of civil disobedience and civil challenge. While definitions of civil disobedience abound,[37] I define civil disobedience as an outward act in direct contravention of a known prohibition or mandate, based on a moral duty to violate that deemed immoral, with the understanding that the immoral prohibition or mandate was government-imposed.[38]

The Movement's track of civil disobedience was theologically based and action-oriented, as many members of the clergy and committed laity defied what they deemed to be unjust laws. For example, to object to laws prohibiting African Americans from eating at public lunch counters in many places in the Deep South, many students and members of the clergy participated in lunch counter sit-ins as a means of civil disobedience.[39]

On the other hand, the track of civil challenge must be distinguished from the track of civil disobedience. Herein, "civil challenge" is defined as legal action within the court system, relying upon the First Amendment's protections to petition government for redress of grievances.[40] Accordingly, the Movement's track of civil challenge was litigious in nature, marked by attorneys working in collaboration with organizations like the NAACP to challenge the constitutionality of unjust laws within the judicial system.[41]

Although the respective tracks of civil disobedience and civil challenge ran parallel courses, they can be reconciled because civil disobedience often led to civil challenge. While the aftermath of Rosa Parks' refusal to give up her bus seat and the Montgomery Bus Boycott, for example, demonstrate how the Movement's acts of civil disobedience ultimately helped shape the First Amendment, the associated lawsuit *Browder v. Gayle* shows how civil disobedience naturally led to civil challenge.[42]

The philosophy of the Movement's civil disobedience—disobeying unjust and discriminatorily enforced laws—was also rooted in the understanding that the First Amendment and the Equal Protection Clause of the Fourteenth Amendment actually supported dissident action. The Movement presented numerous opportunities for clergy and lay activists to shape the First Amendment's broadening scope by forcing the judiciary to address issues such as the public forum,[43] rules governing mass demonstrations,[44] symbolic speech,[45] and freedom of association.[46] Consequently, the Movement's acts of civil disobedience naturally led to civil challenge under the First Amendment and caused the Supreme Court to shape new legal doctrines regulating free speech and free expression.[47] In addressing this presumably unintended consequence, Harvard law professor Randall Kennedy wrote:

> The disciplined peacefulness of the civil rights activists and the underlying decency of their demands helped to create an atmosphere conducive to judicial liberality. The result was not only a beneficial transformation in the substantive law of race relations, but also a blossoming of libertarian themes in First Amendment jurisprudence. In the context of the First Amendment, as in many other areas, the struggle for racial justice produced ramifications that extended far beyond its point of origin. Once loosed, liberty, like equality, was an idea not easily cabined.[48]

On frequent occasions, peaceful protesters attempted to exercise their rights to free speech and assembly as guaranteed by the First Amendment.[49] In a discriminatory fashion, however, the unjust enforcement of laws precluded citizens from doing so. Consequently, much of the Movement's direct action came through the civil disobedience of court-issued injunctions or the administrative denial of permits that would lawfully have allowed activists their First Amendment rights.[50] King's speeches demonstrate his belief that peaceful protest was not only morally permissible, but also a fundamental part of democracy. For example, he stated:

> [T]his is the glory of America, with all of its faults. This is the glory of our democracy. If we were incarcerated behind the iron curtains of a Communistic nation we couldn't do this. If we were trapped in the dungeon of a totalitarian regime we couldn't do this. *But the great glory of American democracy is the right to protest for right.*[51]

While the basic tenets of freedom of speech and freedom of expression were not expressly incorporated into the original Constitution, their omission can arguably be explained by the Framers' belief that the federal government, limited to the powers enumerated in the Constitution, could not enact a law restricting free speech.[52] However, the First Amendment's inclusion in the Bill of Rights is evidence of the Framers' desire to protect freedom of speech and assembly. One media commentator observed:

> [T]he Bill of Rights consists of ten amendments that, like the Constitution itself and the Declaration of Independence before it, are grounded by Natural Law. These ten amendments are designed to protect individual freedoms that the Founders considered

natural rights, thus God-given,
but feared that the new
federal government might
ignore. The Bill of Rights is
supposed to prevent the
federal government from
denying these fundamental
rights to any person. They
reflect human nature in the
absence of a tyrannical
government.[53]

Thus, the First Amendment's express language
demonstrates the Framers' desire to protect the freedoms
enumerated in the amendment.[54] But the events
surrounding the Movement proved to be the first time
these First Amendment rights were enforced with real
force, or given meaning beyond the abstract expression of
them conceptually.

For example, the defiance of unjust laws was at the
heart of *Brown v. Louisiana*,[55] the fourth case in just over
four years, between 1961 and 1966, wherein the Supreme
Court addressed Louisiana statutes prohibiting peaceful
assembly and governmental redress.[56] The *Brown* Court
reversed the convictions of civil rights protesters on the
grounds that they violated the First Amendment and the
Fourteenth Amendment Equal Protection Clause.[57] The
Brown Court's opinion traces the First Amendment's
evolution, especially as it addresses free speech, assembly,
and governmental redress.

The result in *Brown* was rendered within the context
of the facts underlying the lawsuit. On Saturday March 7,
1964, exactly one calendar year before the infamous Bloody
Sunday voting rights march, Henry Brown and four other
Black males participated in a library sit-in at the Clinton,
Louisiana Audubon Regional Library. They were there to
challenge the library's segregationist and discriminatory
practices.[58] After their arrests, the state quickly tried the

protesters and they were found guilty. Under Louisiana's then-existing law, their convictions were not appealable.[59]

After disposing of several preliminary issues dealing with constitutionally infirm actions, the Supreme Court reversed the protesters' convictions and addressed the heart of protected rights under the First and Fourteenth Amendments. In relevant part, the *Brown* Court explained:

> We are here dealing with an aspect of a basic constitutional right—the right under the First and Fourteenth Amendments guaranteeing freedom of speech and of assembly, and freedom to petition the Government for a redress of grievances...As this Court has repeatedly stated, these rights are not confined to verbal expression. They embrace appropriate types of action which certainly include the right in a peaceable and orderly manner to protest by silent and reproachful presence, in a place where the protestant has every right to be, the unconstitutional segregation of public facilities...

> The [Louisiana] statute was deliberately and purposefully applied solely to terminate the reasonable, orderly, and limited exercise of the right to protest the unconstitutional segregation of a public facility.

> Interference with this right, so
> exercised, by state action is
> intolerable under our
> Constitution.[60]

Accordingly, as demonstrated by the events that prompted *Brown*, the Movement helped the Supreme Court broaden the First Amendment's scope by spurring legal actions such as the *Brown* suit.[61]

Just as in *Brown*, in *Edwards v. South Carolina*,[62] a factually similar case, the Supreme Court reached the same conclusion as in *Brown* by reversing the South Carolina state court's conviction of Black citizens for violating the state's peaceful assembly statute.[63] In *Edwards*, a South Carolina magistrate convicted 187 African American high school and college students of violating South Carolina's peaceful assembly laws.[64] After assembling at Columbia's Zion Baptist Church on the morning of March 2, 1961, the petitioners walked at noon in separate groups of approximately fifteen people each to the South Carolina state legislature.[65] Their purpose was to express dissatisfaction with the state's racially discriminatory laws.[66]

After their peaceful and otherwise non-eventful arrival at the state capitol, uniformed police officers told the demonstrators that if they did not disperse, they would be arrested.[67] Rather than dispersing, however, the activists began "listening to a 'religious harangue' by one of their leaders, and loudly singing 'The Star Spangled Banner' and other patriotic and religious songs, while stamping their feet and clapping their hands. After 15 minutes had passed, the police arrested the petitioners and marched them off to jail."[68] Subsequently, the petitioners were convicted in state court for violating the state's peaceful assembly statute, and the South Carolina Supreme Court affirmed the conviction.[69]

In reversing the petitioners' convictions, the U.S. Supreme Court ruled that, "South Carolina infringed the petitioners' constitutionally protected rights of free speech, free assembly, and the freedom to petition for redress of their grievances."[70] Moreover, the Court recognized the nexus between the direct action of the Movement and the First and Fourteenth Amendments, by writing:

> It has long been established that these First Amendment freedoms are protected by the Fourteenth Amendment from invasion by the states...The circumstances in this case reflect an exercise of these basic constitutional rights in their most pristine and classic form. The petitioners felt aggrieved by laws of South Carolina which allegedly "prohibited Negro privileges in this State." They peaceably assembled at the site of the State Government and there peaceably expressed their grievances "to the citizens of South Carolina, along with the Legislative Bodies of South Carolina." Not until they were told by police officials that they must disperse on pain of arrest did they do more. Even then, they but sang patriotic and religious songs after one of their leaders had delivered a "religious harangue." There was no violence or threat of violence on their part, or on

THE KEYS ARE BEING PASSED

the part of any member of the
crowd watching them.[71]

Furthermore, in addressing the relationship between the First and Fourteenth Amendments, the Court also wrote the following:

> The Fourteenth Amendment does not permit a State to make criminal the peaceful expression of unpopular views. A function of free speech under our system of government is to invite dispute. It may indeed best serve its high purpose when it induces a condition of unrest, creates dissatisfaction with conditions as they are, or even stirs people to anger. Speech is often provocative and challenging. It may strike at prejudices and preconceptions and have profound unsettling effects as it presses for acceptance of an idea. That is why freedom of speech...is...protected against censorship or punishment, unless shown likely to produce a clear and present danger of a serious substantive evil that rises far above public inconvenience, annoyance, or unrest...

> There is no room under our Constitution for a more restrictive view. For the alternative would lead to standardization of ideas either by legislatures, courts, or

dominant political or community groups.[72]

Accordingly, the Supreme Court reversed the convictions.[73]

In addition to exemplifying suffering servant theology—a willingness to literally die for the cause in which they believed—the Freedom Riders also had a very significant effect on matters related to the Commerce Clause of the United States Constitution.[74] On June 3, 1946, the Supreme Court decided *Morgan v. Virginia*[75] and held that segregation on buses engaged in interstate commerce violated the Commerce Clause. Further, in December 1960, the Court expanded *Morgan* by opining in *Boynton v. Virginia*[76] that segregation in, *inter alia*, bus terminal waiting rooms and restaurants also violated the Commerce Clause. After the Freedom Riders endured horrific circumstances, on September 22, 1961, the strategy to pursue civil challenge prevailed when the Interstate Commerce Commission ruled that passengers on interstate carriers could be seated without regard to race.[77]

Furthermore, the Commission also ruled that such carriers could not use segregated terminals.[78] The Deep South's reality, however, was that the Court's rulings were ignored. Consequently, with the success of the Montgomery Bus Boycott as the wind at the Movement's back, along with the 1960 election of John F. Kennedy as president of the United States,[79] other nonviolent activists sought to further shape the Movement by achieving full citizenship for all people. In the next wave of nonviolent activities, the Bloody Sunday marchers endured public beatings that put the denial of the right to vote for African Americans front and center for the world. Indeed, the marchers' bloody sacrifice helped expedite the Voting Rights Act of 1965's enactment. In reflecting on that infamous day, Professor David Garrow wrote:

Television footage of the eerie
and gruesome attack produced
immediate national outrage.
King issued a public call for
civil rights supporters across
the nation to come to Selma to
show their support and join a
second attempted march;
congressmen of both parties
called upon President Lyndon
B. Johnson to intervene in
Alabama and to speedily put
voting rights legislation before
Congress. Johnson's Justice
Department aides had already
been hard at work preparing a
comprehensive voting rights
bill, but the "bloody Sunday"
attack and the national
reaction to it spurred the
White House to press for a
faster completion of the
drafting process.[80]

Indeed, for King and other leaders of the Movement,
the Voting Rights Act of 1965 was the promised land of
political and social inclusion that resulted from prolonged
sacrifice and suffering. It was an empirical measure of the
success of civil disobedience and redemptive suffering. In
therefore accepting the dual keys of legacy and
responsibility from the leaders of the Movement, especially
with respect to the hard fought-for right to vote, the
leaders of today's post-modern era should flood the polls on
Election Day. It is simply not enough to vote in large
numbers every four years in presidential election years.
Accepting the keys, from a standpoint of honoring the
sacrifices of those in the Movement leading up to the

Voting Right Act, and carrying forward the commitment to broadening and giving force to the Bill of Rights, means all citizens should work hard to have their voices heard in every democratic election on every social issue. This means voting up or down, yea or nay, on matters like gay marriage, affirmative action, and local tax measures and bond issues. Voting in elections and ensuring others do the same is part of accepting the keys being passed to us by those that have held and tended to them for so long.

Chapter 3

The Fruits of Civil Disobedience:
Passage of the Voting Rights Act of 1965 and
Its Impact on the Movement

Nonviolence is an orphan among
democratic ideas. It has nearly
vanished from public discourse
even though the most basic
element of free government—the
vote—has no other meaning.
Every ballot is a piece of
nonviolence, signifying hard-won
consent to raise politics above
firepower and bloody conquest.
Such compacts work more or less
securely in different lands.
Nations gain strength from vote-
based institutions in commerce
and civil society, but the whole
architecture of representative
democracy springs from the
handiwork of nonviolence.

- Taylor Branch, *At Canaan's Edge*[81]

Although the Movement's leaders had many goals, one
of the Movement's main goals was to achieve full civic
participation without racial discrimination. The enactment
of the Civil Rights Act of 1964[82] and the Voting Rights Act
of 1965 ("VRA")—legislative accomplishments achieved
through civil disobedience—shows the Movement was
indeed successful. Moreover, although both acts were
extremely significant milestones in the Movement's
history, the enactment of the VRA better reflects the

Movement's success because it paved the way for Black political participation in American democracy.[83]

The Movement's leaders recognized that its success would be incomplete unless it resulted in the extension of voting rights to Blacks. For example, Andrew Young, an ordained United Church of Christ minister and one of the Movement's chief lieutenants, who later served as a U.S. ambassador to the United Nations, a member of Congress, and a mayor of Atlanta, writes that "the Civil Rights Act . . . though historic and important, wasn't sufficient without guarantees of the ballot."[84] In discussing the very deliberate decision King and other civil rights activists made to pursue legislation that would protect all citizens' voting rights, it was apparent that the Civil Rights Acts of 1957 and 1960 were simply not enough. Blacks, especially those in the Deep South, needed a specific federal law aimed at protecting the constitutionally provided right to vote.[85] Indeed, prior to the VRA's passage in 1965, the Supreme Court heard numerous cases addressing voting rights violations under applicable provisions of the Civil Rights Acts of 1957 and 1960.[86] These cases proved that case-by-case litigation of voting rights claims under those civil rights laws would only result in incremental and piecemeal gains.[87] Consequently, it was essential that the Movement's religious leaders seek to protect voting rights and that Congress also act to prevent continued discrimination at the polling place.[88] The timing was right and the Movement was poised to draw attention to the drastic problems of racial inequality.

With the Movement well under way, the Bloody Sunday demonstrators only "attempted to draw attention to the political disparities and inequalities [that] blacks were forced to endure because [they] were so frequently denied the right to vote."[89] It worked. On March 15, 1965—just over a week after Bloody Sunday—President Johnson submitted a voting rights bill to Congress, which, under pressure from the Movement, President Johnson and public opinion in the wake of the assassination of Johnson's predecessor, acted pursuant to its constitutional authority[90] and passed the VRA on August 4, 1965.[91] President Johnson signed the VRA into law on August 6 of that year. The theology of civil disobedience had proven successful.

The VRA's passage unquestionably caused significant changes in the United States.[92] In relevant part and of major importance, the VRA contains two "meat and potatoes" provisions, sections 2 and 5. Section 2 applies universally to all jurisdictions and was originally incorporated into the VRA as a restatement of the Fifteenth Amendment.[93] Section 2 prohibits states and political subdivisions within states from instituting any voting qualifications, prerequisites, standards, procedures, or practices in a way that causes the denial or abridgement of the right to vote based on race or color.[94] By contrast, section 5 is considered the heart of the Act,[95] and was arguably the VRA's most important provision, before the U.S. Supreme Court's recent decision in *Shelby County v. Holder*, which struck down Section 4(b) of the VRA and effectively abrogated the provision. Before the *Shelby County* decision, Section 5 applied to only certain covered states and political subdivisions (in other words, "covered jurisdictions"),[96] and required those states and political subdivisions to acquire either judicial or administrative preclearance for any changes to their electoral laws, procedures, or practices.[97] Based on empirical evidence gathered prior to the VRA's enactment, Section 5 was clearly necessary to guarantee the opportunity and right for Blacks to participate in the electoral process in the covered jurisdictions.[98]

Although the Thirteenth, Fourteenth, and Fifteenth Amendments to the United States Constitution ended involuntary servitude, granted Blacks full citizenship, and theoretically granted the right to vote, the Amendments' practical effect was far less functional. Louisiana, for example, has a long history of *de jure* and *de facto* restrictions on the right of Black citizens to register, vote, and otherwise participate in the democratic process. The VRA, therefore, set its sights on the most visible barriers to Black legal equality. These barriers were defined primarily as direct, formal discriminatory practices intended to exclude Black participation in the central political and economic institutions of American life.

From its inception, the United States has had a bitterly long history of racial divisiveness. Consequently, even though Blacks were "free" to vote after adoption of the Fifteenth Amendment, states continued to deny minority citizens this fundamental right. Moreover, as other commentators have noted in addressing the necessity of federal legislation to protect minority citizens' right to vote:

> Litigation of voting rights claims on a case-by-case basis under the Civil Rights Acts of 1957, 1960, and 1964 attempted to remedy unconstitutional voting practices but had only negligible success, result[ing] in only piecemeal gains...and was thwarted by the development of new voting practices abridging or denying the minority right to vote.[99]

It was therefore essential that Congress pass federal legislation to prevent discrimination at the polling place.[100]

In *Lane v. Wilson*,[101] U.S. Supreme Court Justice Felix Frankfurter observed that the Fifteenth Amendment "nullifies sophisticated as well as simple-minded modes of discrimination. It hits onerous procedural requirements which effectively handicap exercise of the franchise . . ."[102] Despite the broad intentions of the amendment, however, "white [s]outherners in charge of registration and voting readily circumvented the Fifteenth Amendment. They had an arsenal of discriminatory schemes."[103]

Notwithstanding flagrant attempts to limit minority citizens' power of the franchise,

> [T]he Voting Rights Act is one of the most successful civil rights statutes ever passed by Congress. The [A]ct accomplished what the Fifteenth Amendment to the U.S. Constitution and numerous federal statutes had failed to accomplish—it provided minority voters an opportunity to participate in the electoral process and elect candidates of their choice, generally free of discrimination.[104]

The VRA was so successful in addressing historic disenfranchisement because it essentially shifted responsibility for ensuring that the right to vote was not abridged from the courts to the United States Department of Justice.[105] A big part of the responsibility shifting was due to the application of Section 2 of the VRA, which eliminated voter qualifications as prerequisites to voting.[106]

Section 2 and its Evolution

Section 2 of the VRA, as originally passed in 1965, provided as follows:

> No voting qualification or prerequisite to voting, or standard, practice, or procedure shall be imposed or applied by any State or political subdivision to deny the right of any citizen of the United States to vote on account of

race or color, or in contravention of the guarantees set forth in section 1973b (f)(2) of this title.

Thus, it was originally a restatement of the Fifteenth Amendment and applies to all jurisdictions. It prohibits any state or political subdivision from imposing a "voting qualification or prerequisite to voting or standard, practice or procedure . . . in a manner which results in the denial or abridgment of the right to vote on account of race or color." Stated otherwise:

> [T]he Act was viewed by many southern African-Americans and civil rights activists as the resurrection of the [F]ifteenth [A]mendment, a provision rendered impotent prior to the passage of the Act by discrimination. For more than a half century, white-controlled governments in the South had suppressed the minority right to vote through the use of violence, intimidation, and devices such as literacy tests, poll taxes, and primaries restricted on the basis of race and wealth.[107]

In 1982, Congress amended the VRA to infuse it with new life in response to the Supreme Court's ruling in *City of Mobile v. Bolden*.[108] In *Bolden*, a group of Black citizens alleged Mobile's practice of electing commissioners at-large illegally diluted minority voting strength, thus violating the Fourteenth and Fifteenth Amendments and Section 2 of the VRA. The Court's plurality opinion provided that "racially discriminatory motivation is a necessary ingredient of a Fifteenth Amendment violation."[109]

Moreover, the Court concluded the plaintiffs failed to prove a violation under Section 2 of the VRA because Congress did not intend Section 2 to have any effect different from that of the Fifteenth Amendment.

The *Bolden* Court reasoned that Section 2 only operated to prohibit intentionally discriminatory acts by state officials. Subsequent analysis has noted:

> [T]he Court required proof of discriminatory intent for claims brought under [S]ection 2 of the...Act, as well as those brought under the [F]ourteenth and [F]ifteenth [A]mendments. Under this new, onerous burden of proof, plaintiffs could no longer rely on proof of discriminatory effect to raise an inference of intent; they now had to prove discriminatory purpose by "direct, smoking gun evidence."[110]

Accordingly, under the Court's holding, "[a]bsent direct evidence of invidious purpose, no multimember electoral systems could be challenged under either the Constitution or the Voting Rights Act."[111]

Congress amended Section 2 to eliminate proof of intent as a requirement to establish a violation of the statute.[112] By doing so, "Congress adopted the 'results' test, whereby plaintiffs may prevail under [S]ection 2 by demonstrating that under the totality of the circumstances, a challenged election law or procedure has the effect of denying or abridging the right to vote on the basis of race."[113] Therefore it is clear that Congress "amended the Voting Rights Act expressly to repudiate *Bolden* and to outlaw electoral practices that 'result in' the denial of equal political opportunity to minority groups."[114]

The U.S. Senate Judiciary Committee found the *Bolden*

Court "had broken with precedent and substantially increased the burden on plaintiffs in voting discrimination cases by requiring proof of discriminatory intent."[115] As such, the committee's report concluded "[t]his intent test places an unacceptably difficult burden on plaintiffs. It divests the judicial injury [sic] from the crucial question of whether minorities have equal access to the electoral process to a historical question of individual motives."[116] The committee's report also took from *Zimmer v. McKeithen*[117] a non-exhaustive list of factors for courts to consider as part of Section 2's legislative history.[118]

Since the Congressional amendment in 1982, Section 2 reads:

> No voting qualification or prerequisite to voting or standard, practice, or procedure shall be imposed or applied by any State or political subdivision in a manner which results in a denial or abridgment of the right of any citizen of the United States to vote on account of race or color, or in contravention of the guarantees set forth in section 1973(f)(2) of this title, as provided in subsection (b) of this section.
>
> A violation of subsection (a) is established if, based on the totality of the circumstances, it is shown that the political process leading to nomination or election in the State or political subdivision are not equally open to participation by members of a class of citizens protected by subsection (a) of this section in that its members have

less opportunity than other members of the electorate to participate in the political process. And to elect representatives of their choice. The extent to which members of a protected class have been elected to office in the State or political subdivision is one circumstance which may be considered: *Provided*, That nothing in this section establishes a right to have members of a protected class elected in numbers equal to their proportion in the population.[119]

In 1984, the first case challenging at-large judicial elections under Section 2 of the Act was filed in the United States District Court for the District of Southern Mississippi.[120] Between 1982 and 1986, several lower court decisions upheld the constitutionality of the VRA's 1982 Amendments.[121] However, the U.S. Supreme Court first considered the VRA's 1982 amendments in the 1986 case *Thornburg v. Gingles.*[122]

In *Gingles*, the plaintiffs challenged North Carolina's 1982 redistricting plans for one multimember state senate district, one single-member state senate district, and five multimember state house districts. Pursuant to Section 5 of the VRA, the Department of Justice precleared the districts. The plaintiffs, however, alleged the precleared districts impaired Black citizens' ability to elect representatives of their choice, in violation of the Fourteenth and Fifteenth Amendments and Section 2 of the VRA.

In writing for the Court, Justice Brennan analyzed the legislative history of Section 2 and rejected the earlier test of intent to discriminate and instead noted that in determining if a Section 2 violation has occurred, the courts should decide whether "as a result of the challenged practice or structure plaintiffs do not have an equal opportunity to participate in the political processes and to elect candidates of their choice."[123] Brennan further indicated that a court "must assess the impact of the contested structure or practice on minority electoral opportunities 'on the basis of objective factors.'"[124]

Furthermore, in addition to the "objective factor" analysis, the *Gingles* Court developed a new three-part test that a minority group must meet to establish a vote dilution claim under Section 2 of the VRA. The test requires that a minority group prove: (1) it is sufficiently large and geographically compact to constitute a majority in a single-member district; (2) it is politically cohesive; and (3) in the absence of special circumstances, block voting by the white majority usually defeats the minority's preferred candidate. The *Gingles* test remains the applicable test in Section 2 dilution cases to this day.

Section 5 and its Evolution

Like Section 2, Section 5 has also undergone amendments since it was enacted in 1965. More recently, the Supreme Court's *Shelby County v. Holder* decision has effectively placed its enforcement on hold until a new coverage formula is developed to replace the former Section 4(b) formula that the *Shelby County* opinion struck down.

When the VRA was originally passed, Section 5 was considered one of the primary enforcement mechanisms to ensure that minority voters would have an opportunity to register to vote and fully participate in the electoral process free of discrimination. Moreover, the intent of Section 5 was to prevent states that had a history of racially discriminatory electoral practices from developing new and innovative means to continue to disenfranchise Black voters.

Before Congress passed the VRA in 1965, Congress had already passed several laws attempting to protect minority citizens. Nevertheless, as noted by the U.S Supreme Court, "despite the earnest efforts of the Justice Department and of many federal judges...laws [did] little to cure the problem of vot[er] discrimination."[125] Before Congress passed Section 5, "the federal government, through the Civil Rights Division of the Department of Justice undertook the arduous and time-consuming task of filing individual suits against each discriminatory voting law, based on the Civil Rights Acts of 1957 and 1960. This approach proved unsuccessful in increasing Black voter registration."[126] In contrast, another reason the VRA proved so effective was the requirements within Section 5.

Section 5 requires that covered jurisdictions submit any proposed changes in voting qualification or prerequisite to voting, or standard, practice or procedure with respect to voting to either the U.S. Department of Justice or the U.S. District Court for the District of Columbia for preclearance before the proposed change can be implemented. If a covered jurisdiction seeks pre-clearance through the courts, the preclearance is considered "judicial." Conversely, if the jurisdiction seeks pre-clearance through the Department of Justice, it is considered "administrative."

In 1970, Congress amended Section 5 by extending the preclearance requisite of Section 5 for an additional five years. In 1975, Congress amended it again to extend the section's preclearance requirements for an additional seven years, or through the 1980 redistricting cycle. In 1982, Congress again extended the section's preclearance requirements for an additional twenty-five years, through 2007. With regard to covered jurisdictions, therefore, the preclearance requirements of Section 5 were almost absolute.

The 1975 amendments also added the required use of bilingual election materials and assistance if five percent of the jurisdiction's voting age citizens were of a single language minority and the literacy rate of that language minority group was greater than the national average.

Furthermore, the 1975 amendments expanded the coverage requirements of Section 5 to include jurisdictions that maintained any test or device and had less than half of their voting age population either registered on November 1, 1972 or voting in the November 1972 federal election. Because the 1982 amendments only extended Section 5's preclearance requirement an additional twenty-five years, they did not make any substantive changes to the section.

In addition to the Congress' actions in amending the VRA, the Supreme Court has been active in interpreting it. For example, in *Beer v. United States*, the Supreme Court addressed the issue of whether changes in the apportionment of city council districts in the city of New Orleans ("the City") violated the VRA. The City conducted its standard decennial reapportionment after it received the figures from the 1970 Census. When the City attempted to obtain administrative preclearance of its reapportionment from the U.S. Department of Justice, however, the attorney general rejected the City's plans as impermissibly diluting Black voting strength by combining a number of Back voters with a larger number of white voters. The City, therefore, filed a petition with the U.S. District Court for the District of Columbia, pursuant to Section 5 of the VRA, seeking judicial preclearance of its newly adopted city council reapportionment plan. Like the Department of Justice, the district court found the City's new reapportionment plan would abridge the voting rights of the City's Black citizens and concluded, "Plan II would have the effect of abridging the right to vote on account of race or color."[127] Accordingly, the district court dismissed the City's suit, denying preclearance.

On appeal, the Supreme Court reversed and remanded.[128] The Supreme Court found the City's new reapportionment plan was valid where it had the effect of enhancing the position of racial minorities. In reversing the lower court, the Supreme Court noted "[t]he language of § 5 clearly provides that *it applies only to proposed changes in voting procedures. '[D]iscriminatory practices...instituted prior to November 1964...are not subject to the requirement of preclearance [under § 5].'*"[129] Moreover, the Court wrote, "[a] new legislative apportionment cannot violate § 5 unless the new apportionment itself so discriminates on the basis of race or color as to violate the Constitution."[130]

In 1983, the Supreme Court broadened the *Beer* Court's retrogression standard in *City of Lockhart v. United States.*[131] In *Lockhart*, the Supreme Court approved preclearance of an electoral change that did not improve the position of minority voters. The Supreme Court noted, however, that "[a]lthough there may have been no improvement in [minority] voting strength, there has been no retrogression, either."[132] Accordingly, the Supreme Court reasoned that "[s]ince the new plan did not increase the degree of discrimination against [B]lacks, it was entitled to preclearance."

Justice Thurgood Marshall, the Court's only Black member, dissented in *Lockhart*. Justice Marshall wrote that "[b]y holding that § 5 forbids only electoral changes that *increase* discrimination, the Court reduces § 5 to a means of maintaining the status quo."[133] Marshall therefore reasoned the Supreme Court's view would permit the adoption of a discriminatory electoral scheme, provided the scheme was no more discriminatory than its predecessor and was consistent with both the language and intent of Section 5.

In another case, *Young,*[134] the Supreme Court specifically addressed the question of whether changes the state of Mississippi made to the procedure by which its residents and citizens were allowed to register to vote—changes made to be in compliance with the National Voter Registration Act of 1993 ("NVRA")—required preclearance under Section 5. The Court began from the position that all electoral changes, regardless of the reason therefore, must be precleared by covered jurisdictions. Accordingly, the Court expressly ruled that Mississippi's compliance with the NVRA was subject to the requirements under Section 5.

The NVRA requires states to provide simplified systems for registering to vote in federal elections. In accordance with the NVRA, states must provide a system for voter registration by mail, at various state offices, and on a driver's license application. In an effort to comply with the statute, the state of Mississippi made certain changes in its registration procedures. The changes were subsequently challenged by four private plaintiffs in the United States district court and consolidated with a similar matter filed by the United States. The three-judge district court granted the defendant's dispositive motion and rejected the plaintiffs' argument. The district court essentially rejected plaintiffs' arguments by reasoning that because the changes at issue were an attempt to correct a misapplication of state law, they consequently did not require preclearance under Section 5 of the NVRA.

Discussing the critical nature of Section 5's preclearance provision(s) in all instances when a covered jurisdiction makes any changes to voter and voting practices or procedures, the Supreme Court reversed the district court's ruling. In generally discussing the absolute necessity of preclearance, the Court wrote:

> [P]reclearance is, in effect, a determination that the change "does not have the purpose and will not have the effect of denying or abridging the right to vote on account of race or color." In the language of § 5 jurisprudence, this determination involves a determination that the change is not retrogressive.[135]

Furthermore, in specifically examining the issues in *Young*, the Court went on to hold the following:

> The problem for Mississippi is that
> preclearance typically requires
> examination of discretionary changes
> in context—a context that includes
> history, purpose, and practical
> effect...The applicants and the
> [g]overnment argue...the particular
> changes and the way Mississippi
> administers them *could*...abridge the
> right to vote. We cannot say whether
> or not that is so, for that is an
> argument for the merits. The
> question here is "preclearance," and
> preclearance is necessary so that the
> appellants and the [g]overnment will
> have the opportunity to find out if it
> is true.[136]

The Court reversed the district court's grant of summary judgment against the plaintiffs. It also remanded the litigation, directing the state of Mississippi to preclear the changes it made to be in compliance with the NVRA.[137]

By precipitating Black voter registration gains and targeting discriminatory election techniques, the VRA gave southern Blacks in small towns and rural communities their first opportunity to meaningfully participate in the American electoral process. Even in places that were not "covered jurisdictions,"[138] African Americans achieved significant firsts with election to offices never before held by Blacks. For example, in 1967, Richard Hatcher and Carl Stokes, elected as mayor of Gary, Indiana, and Cleveland, Ohio, respectively, became the first African American mayors of major cities.[139] Without question, their successful elections, followed in succession by many Black candidates across the United States, showed that the Movement had progressed from "protest to politics."[140] The VRA has also resulted in more long-term political gains. In

Louisiana, for example, as of 2006, 20.8% of the state court judges were African American, compared with 4.8%, 3.5%, and 9.3% in America's three largest states: California, Texas, and New York, respectively.[141] Moreover, the resulting changes would continually be seen over decades to come in such cities as New Orleans, Atlanta, Detroit, Los Angeles, Seattle, and New York.[142] As a testament to the Act's continued effectiveness, and in tribute to the Movement, Congress reauthorized the VRA in 2006.[143]

The VRA's Uncertain Future

The effectiveness of the VRA has led to recent challenges based on the argument that the VRA has been so effective in its mission that it is no longer necessary to address past disenfranchisement in covered jurisdictions. For example, just years after Congress's 2006 VRA reauthorization, the Supreme Court was called upon to address Section 5's constitutionality in *Northwest Austin Municipal Utility District No. 1 v. Holder*.[144] Instead of doing so, however, the Supreme Court resolved the dispute by reversing the appealed decision on the basis of an issue other than Section 5's validity. Accordingly, although Section 5 remains "alive," an argument can be made that it may not be "well."

In *Holder*, the petitioner was a small utility district with an elected board that was required to seek preclearance under section 5 before it could change anything related to its elections.[145] The utility district sought judicial preclearance by seeking relief under the Act's "bailout provision" in the VRA's section 4,[146] asserting that it should be released from preclearance because it met certain requirements.[147] Alternatively, the utility district argued if Section 5 were interpreted to render it ineligible for Section 4's bailout, section 5 was unconstitutional. The federal district court rejected both claims, opining the utility district was not eligible for

Section 4's bailout and, considering the extensive and comprehensive legislative history associated with the Act's 2006 reauthorization,[148] Section 5's twenty-five year extension was indeed constitutional. The utility district appealed.[149]

In noting the *Holder* litigation's significance, yet deciding to resolve the matter by means other than looking at section 5's constitutionality, the Supreme Court wrote:

> That constitutional question has attracted ardent briefs from dozens of interested parties, but the importance of the question does not justify our rushing to decide it. Quite the contrary: Our usual practice is to avoid the unnecessary resolution of constitutional questions. We agree that the district is eligible under the Act to seek bailout. We therefore reverse, and do not reach the constitutionality of § 5.[150]

Most recently, in its 2013 opinion, *Shelby County v. Holder,* the Supreme Court agreed with Shelby County, Alabama's argument that the effectiveness of the VRA had rendered the coverage formula in Section 4(b) obsolete, given the significant gains African Americans have made in ability to exercise their vote since the enactment of the VRA. The Supreme Court declined to strike down the Section 5 preclearance provisions, but rendered the provisions in Section 5 inapplicable unless and until Congress develops an updated Section 4(b) coverage formula that comports with the present situation in American political districts.

Consequently, the VRA continues to survive, in that the Supreme Court's "look" at Section 5 so far has only been a look away. In analyzing the two most recent opinions on the VRA the Supreme Court has rendered, then, it appears that the gains of the Movement realized with the enactment of the VRA are, 50 years after its enactment, in serious jeopardy.[151]

In this regard, in the face of the recent Supreme Court rulings on the constitutionality of the VRA, and given the resulting push forward on voter suppression efforts in formerly covered jurisdictions, such as Texas' Voter ID Act, which was enacted just days after the Supreme Court's ruling in *Shelby County v. Holder*, accepting the keys for the next generation of civil rights leaders means being vigilant. Those who would accept the keys must be ever on the look out for changes to electoral laws that would push the people back into the situation of voter suppression and discriminatory disenfranchisement that made the enactment of the VRA necessary less than a century ago. It would be a travesty to allow the gains of the Movement in this area to slip away because of inattention of the very beneficiaries of the efforts of the courageous and selfless people who fought to obtain those gains.

Chapter 4

The Keys Are Being Passed

(A Sermon for Martin Luther King, Jr. Day at St. Paul AME Church in New Orleans)

Now when Jesus came into the district of Caesarea Philippi, he asked his disciples, "Who do people say that the Son of Man is?" And they said, "Some say John the Baptist, but others Elisha, and still others Jeremiah or one of the prophets." He said to them, "But who do you say that I am?" Simon Peter answered, "You are the Messiah, the Son of the living God." And Jesus answered him, "Blessed are you Simon, son of Jonah! For flesh and blood has not revealed this to you, but my Father in heaven. And I tell you, you are Peter, and on this rock, I will build <u>my church,</u> and the gates of Hades will not prevail against it. <u>I will give you the keys of the kingdom of heaven,</u> and whatever you bind on earth, will be bound in heaven, and whatever you loose on earth shall be loosed in heaven."

- *Matthew* 16:13-19 (NRSV)(emphasis added)

Giving someone keys symbolizes giving them authority and responsibility. It also symbolizes ushering in something new. Passing keys, therefore, is about transitioning a legacy and also passing responsibility.

When I was a boy, growing up in New Orleans, I can remember when my mother gave me the keys to our house. It was sort of a rite of passage and I can remember the seriousness of the moment. She said "Son, I expect you to come home after school and start your homework." I said, "Yes, mama." She said, "Son, I expect you to keep this place clean." I said, "Yes, mama." And she said, "Jonathan, you better not have any little girls in this house!!!!" I said, "Yes, mama! I understand." My mother giving me the keys was special because it symbolized her giving me responsibility and, in a way, legacy as I was being welcomed into adulthood.

The semester I completed my seminary studies, I was required to do an intercultural immersion trip. It just so happens that the trip scheduled that semester was to Italy. Of all the wonderful things we did during those 10 days in Italy, the most memorable thing for me came while in Rome, visiting the Vatican. Along with several other seminarians, I had been down in the basement of the Vatican, the Grottoes, and seen where all the previous popes are buried. Indeed, because the Vatican is at St. Peter's Square, at the very center of the Grottoes and at ground zero is Peter's remains. Our Catholic brothers and sisters literally built Jesus' church on St. Peter!

After having been through centuries of some of the most beautiful art known to mankind, and spending more than an hour looking at the beauty of the Sistine Chapel, I was with a group that walked out of the Vatican's front door. We were all sort of on circuit overload, amazed at the wonders we had just seen. As I was leaning on a rail, literally at the center of the front door to the Vatican, a friend of mine said "Look up. Do you think that's real gold?" He was pointing to a marble carving of Jesus, with disciples standing around him, and one disciple, Peter, kneeling before him. Jesus was giving Peter a set of golden keys. In addition to giving Peter authority, Jesus was also transitioning to give him the legacy of Judaism while simultaneously creating something new, the church.

When we look at the text, we see the scriptural basis for that beautiful marble carving. Jesus was passing on the keys. Much like the time my mother gave me the keys to our house, Jesus was passing on his trust and giving Peter authority over something that was precious to him, his faith! In order to appreciate the text, and to apply it broadly to the celebration of our Martin Luther King, Jr. Worship Service, we can't look at the text in a vacuum. The text is part of a larger story. Therefore, to talk about the text, I want to take you on a trip that I like to call "a loop." After laying a foundation for the loop, I want to talk about: (1) the "transition" in the text; (2) the "transition" in our world; (3) I want to then talk about God's grace and God's movement in the text; and (4) I want to bring us home by talking about God's grace and God's movement in the world. If we do this thing right, we'll end ready to accept the keys of legacy and responsibility that are being passed to us all as beneficiaries of Dr. King's work in the Movement.

In order to appreciate the text, we have to lay a foundation. The text doesn't just appear in a vacuum. It is part of a larger story of God's chosen people and God choosing us as members of God's church. First of all, when we look at the *Gospel of Matthew*, it is considered by many theologians to be the "gospel of the church." *Matthew* is a transitional narrative that bridges the past with the future. Although *Matthew* is the first book of the New Testament cannon, it is not the first book written in the New Testament. The first New Testament writing was actually Paul's epistle we know as *First Thessalonians*. Moreover, the oldest of the gospel narrative is actually *Mark*. Why then does Matthew begin the New Testament?

In the Old Testament, we are introduced to "Messianic Scriptures," or scriptures that tell of the coming of the Messiah. God makes the children of Israel a promise, called the "Davidic Covenant," that the messiah will come from the House of David. As the New Testament transitions to gives us Jesus, the writer of *Matthew* is the only gospel writer that begins his narrative with a genealogical account of the paternal ancestry of Jesus, thus authenticating the promise made and showing Jesus is indeed the foretold messiah.

Matthew also transitions by introducing something new. Although *Matthew* shows great continuity with Jewish tradition and custom, *Matthew* also ushers in a revolutionary term: "the church." We haven't seen anything about "the church" in the entire Bible, prior to its use in *Matthew*. In the Old Testament, for example, consistent with Jewish culture, we see the construction of King Solomon's temple. Even with Jesus in the New Testament, the gospel writers tell us the story of Jesus staying behind as a boy in the Jewish synagogue. For the first time in the entire Bible, *Matthew* shows the reader Jesus breaking with the past and transitioning into something new, when he uses the term "the church." He's passing on the keys to Peter to build "the church."

When we look at the text, we see a certain transition of the old giving way to the new. Jesus is not commissioning Peter to build another synagogue or another temple; instead, Jesus is commissioning Peter to build something entirely new, while using the foundation of what he has. He's ushering in a Judeo-Christian faith by commissioning Peter to build the church. It is Peter's faith that allows him to build on the old by establishing something new. When Jesus asks Peter, "Who do you say that I am," Peter responds by indicating that Jesus is the messiah. In other words, Peter is showing transition by proclaiming that Jesus is the fulfillment of the promise God made generations and generations ago to the people of Israel, through King David. Jesus is "the one" that would come to bring reconciliation and restore humankind with God. The transition in the text, therefore, is Peter bridging the gap between the old and the new. When the new comes, it must build on the old, not disregard it.

Last year, I was with some friends in Shreveport for the groundbreaking of a new charter school. As I was with some in the education community, we were joking about the transition from the "old" to the "new." Someone told a story about a teacher who was asking one of her students where he could find out more about the lesson they were discussing. The teacher then said that she'd like the student to go to the library and look it up in an encyclopedia. The student was puzzled. He asked the teacher if by "encyclopedia," she meant "Wikipedia?" In other words, there's been a change or a transition. But, just because there's something new, we don't throw the baby out with the bathwater. We build on the old with the keys of legacy and responsibility to usher in the new.

When I was a boy, I can remember by father taking pride in buying sets of encyclopedias for our house because he wanted his children to have books! Today, however, I wouldn't know where to buy encyclopedias or if people still sell them. I do know that when my nine-year-old daughter, Jillian, had questions about an assignment, she used her iPad and came back to tell me about Newton's Laws of Gravity. In other words, the "new" transitions by building on the "old." That's what Jesus was doing by passing the keys to Peter. He was building on "the old," but ushering in "the new." That's the transition in the text.

There is also a similar transition in the world. Transition may be ceremonial—like Jesus giving Peter the keys—or it might be, in the words of our departed brother Malcolm, "By Any Means Necessary!"

As we reflect on the legacy of Martin Luther King, Jr. and observe the fiftieth (50th) anniversary of the Movement, we are forced to recall that many of the stories we celebrate were not so ceremonious. For example, in 2012 and 2013, we celebrated the reelection and inauguration of America's 44th president, the Honorable Barack Obama. Let us not forget though, that the election of a Black president in America was only made possible by

55

the people who were victim to violent attacks by dogs, suffering the humility of being beaten to within an inch of their lives, while crossing the Edmund Pettis Bridge in Selma, Alabama and marching with God as their comforter because they wanted passage of the Voting Rights Act. That's an example of transition in the world and an example of how the keys were passed from King to Obama.

Let us not forget that on the same day we celebrated the inauguration of President Barack Obama, we also observed the birthday of our departed brother, Martin Luther King. If you really want to celebrate the legacy of Dr. King and how the keys are being passed from his generation on, don't just remember the sunlight of the many in the March on Washington. You've got to also remember the darkness of solitude in that jail cell in Alabama where King was locked up for exercising his constitutional right of free assembly and pieced together, on napkins, the twentieth century's most prolific treatise on civil disobedience, *Letter From Birmingham Jail.* In other words, we've got to remember the tough times in order to accept responsibility for the keys that are being passed to us all. When I was a young boy, I can remember my mother offering words of encouragement by saying, "Son, if you work hard and pray, you can be anything that you want to be." I think it is wonderful for a parent to encourage their child, but I don't know if in the 1970s—if deep inside—my mother really believed the encouragement she offered. Today, however, since the keys are being passed as part of King's legacy, and opportunities are extended to this generation of leaders, let us not forget that the 2008 election of Barack Obama was so historic because 150 years ago, Obama's ancestors were set free from the shackles of slavery by the stroke of a pen in President Lincoln signing the *Emancipation Proclamation.* Now, since the keys are being passed, as a result of Obama's historic election, we transitioned from Kennedy to Johnson and Carter to Clinton by writing history with the first African-American president of the United States of

America. Now, we can truly look our children in the eyes and encourage them with the confidence of knowing they can really be anything they want to be. That's part of the transition in the world that we celebrate as the legacy of Martin Luther King. What I'm trying to say is that the keys are being passed.

Now although King was a graduate of Morehouse College, Crozier Divinity School, and earned a PhD from Boston University, at his core, King was a product of and a minister in the Black church. The Black church, I would argue, is different from mainline churches because part of the keys of legacy and responsibility of the Black church is not just to deal with salvation in the "kingdom to come." It's also to deal with the inequities of the "kingdom at hand." That's what I like to call "the social gospel."

Just as in today's text, Jesus passes the keys on to Peter by building on the foundation of Judaism and creating something new—the legacy of the Christian church—King also passes the keys on to us by building on the legacy of Jesus' church and ushering in the legacy of the social gospel. Those are the keys to the Black church. In other words, as part of King's legacy, the Black church uses the Christian cross for something good. It's not just about salvation. It's also about service. The vertical and horizontal planes of the cross must exist together.

As history shows us, we have to be careful with some people that use the cross. The Ku Klux Klan uses the cross. If you just emphasize the vertical plane of the cross, the up and down axis of the cross, you have a stick. You can do lots of harm with a stick. You can beat and oppress people with a stick. Similarly, you can't just emphasize the cross' horizontal plane that represents social outreach and community good. If you just have the horizontal plane, you have a social club that does no good for others in need. But, if you use both planes of the cross, recognizing the vertical is about individual salvation and the horizontal is about community engagement, you're then practicing the social gospel that distinguishes the Black church. To put it in the words of Dr. King, from his first book, *Stride Toward Freedom*, consider it like this:

> [T]he Christian gospel is a two-way road. On the one hand, it seeks to change the souls of men, and thereby unite them with God; on the other hand, it seeks to change the environmental conditions of men so that the soul will have a chance after it is changed. Any religion that professes to be concerned with the souls of men and is not concerned with the slums that damn them, the economic conditions that strangle them, and the social conditions that cripple them is a dry-as-dust religion.

- Martin Luther King, Jr., *Stride Toward Freedom*

As an ordained minister in the African Methodist Episcopal Church, when I think about the legacy of the Black church and the social gospel of the Black church, I believe community outreach *is* the social gospel and the social gospel should come through the Black church. That's what Dr. King was all about. Church can't just deal with salvation in the "kingdom to come." Church has also got to deal with the inequities of the "kingdom at hand." Our role is to accept the keys that are being passed and recommit ourselves to Dr. King's legacy of service. After all, the keys are being passed.

We have talked about the transition in the text and the transition in the word; let's talk for a moment about

God's grace and God's movement in the text before looking at God's grace and God's movement in our lives.

When we look at the text, Jesus is making a way out of no way to establish the church. Remember, the text doesn't appear in a vacuum. It's part of a larger story. The text builds on the "old" by ushering in the "new" to also establish salvation. Indeed, it is through Jesus and Jesus' church that we experience God's unmerited gift of salvation. God is moving in the text by calling victory for all those who are a part of the church. The text says "the gates of Hades will not prevail against Jesus' church." In other words, Jesus is declaring victory for the church and the anticipated fulfillment of the Davidic Covenant because the members of the church will be reconciled in relationship with God, because of Jesus.

One of the core beliefs in Methodism, if you look at our Articles of Religion, is the belief in ancestral or original sin. In other words, the Old Testament Genesis narrative tells us about "A-dam," a term which is generic for man or mankind, and mankind's act of original sin. Because of that act of original sin, we believe that all humans born thereafter were subject to commit sin because they just couldn't help themselves. Because of original sin, therefore, humans were relegated to a place of eternal separation from the grace of God. Something had to be done. God loves humanity too much to just let the madness go on and the mess keep piling up. As God's solution to the madness, we believe God became incarnate in the person of Jesus and paid the debt for human error so we could all experience salvation. That's what I call GRACE.

The text shows Jesus giving Peter—and all human beings, I believe—the authority associated with the keys. The text says whatever you bind on earth will be bound in heaven and whatever you loose on earth will be loosed in heaven. In other words, thank God for giving us an opportunity to experience salvation...Thank God for giving us the precious gift of salvation ...Thank God for building on the old and giving us something new...Thank God for making a way out of no way! That's the movement of God in the text! The movement results in the creation of what we celebrate today: Jesus' church. That's the symbolism of the keys Jesus gives to Peter.

Now, just as God creates something new in the text with the commission of Peter to build Jesus' church, God has also commissioned others to make a way out of no way, too. In fact, history tells us that God commissions or "calls" some of those that are the most unlikely candidates to do God's work. The symbolic passing of the keys, therefore, means that when God calls you...when God commissions you...when God gives you authority...when God gives you the keys . . . you can indeed make a way out of no way and prevail against any and all obstacles that the gates of Hades might place in your way.

Somehow I believe that if we could ask Thurgood Marshall about his relationship with God, he'd tell us that God gave him the keys to the courthouse so he could takedown Jim Crow segregation in public education. The keys are being passed. That's why we have more Black administrators and superintendents in school districts all across America.

Somehow I believe that if we could ask Arthur Ashe about his relationship with God, he'd tell us that God gave him the keys to the country club so he could open the gates for Venus and Serena to get their boogie on at Wimbledon and young black girls would play tennis like never before.

Somehow I believe that if we could ask Rosa Parks about her relationship with God, she'd tell us that God gave her the keys to a local bus in Montgomery, Alabama so we could all travel in interstate commerce throughout the United States of America.

Somehow I believe that if we could ask Ralph Bunche about his relationship with God, he'd tell us that God gave him the keys to international diplomacy so Colin Powell and Condoleezza Rice could serve as African American Secretaries of State.

Somehow I believe that if we could ask Shirley Chisholm about her relationship with God, she'd say that

God gave her the keys to be the first African American to run for the presidency, in 1972, so Barack Obama could win in 2008. Each and every time you vote in an election, you celebrate the fact that the keys are being passed! Each and every time you "do unto others as you would have them do unto you," you affirm yourself as a member of Jesus' church and celebrate the fact that the keys are being passed!

There's no time to say, "Mama, I'm not ready for the responsibility of having my own set of keys. Can you pick me up from school?" There's no saying "Time out!" The keys are being passed. Each and every time you pray and thank Jesus for all he's done, you must recommit yourself to serving others, just like Jesus did. Those are the keys that King's legacy gives to us all. We must celebrate the fact that the keys are being passed! The keys are being passed, my brothers and sisters! The keys are being passed!

PART TWO

Law, Religion and Environmental Justice

THE KEYS ARE BEING PASSED

Chapter 5

The Origins of Environmental Justice: The Holy Bible

Then I saw a new heaven and a new earth; for the first heaven and the first earth had passed away, and the sea was no more. And I saw the holy city, the New Jerusalem, coming down out of heaven from God, prepared as a bride adorned for her husband. And I heard a loud voice from the throne saying, "See, the home of God is among mortals. He will dwell with them as their God; they will be his peoples, and God himself will be with them; he will wipe out every tear from their eyes . . ." Then he said to me, "It is done! I am the Alpha and the Omega, the beginning and the end. To the thirsty, I will give water as a gift from the spring of the water of life."

- Book of Revelation (NRSV)[152]

The environmental justice movement, an outgrowth of the Movement, began with committed and socially conscience clergy demanding better conditions for marginalized Blacks. Just as the original Movement began with committed clergy demanding equal rights and justice for those pushed to the periphery, and doing so because of deeply rooted Judeo-Christian ideals about love and equality, the environmental justice movement also began with its foundations in the church—specifically in the *Book of Revelation* (*Revelation*). Indeed, *Revelation* calls upon Judeo-Christian practitioners, including President Barack Obama, to be wise stewards of the planet Earth.

President Obama's administration has placed an emphasis on "environmental justice."[153] His administration has pushed for and funded "green" projects and research into alternative "renewable" energy sources that result in less pollution to the surrounding environment when used. Notwithstanding his administration's environmental policy focus, the term environmental justice remains inherently ambiguous—implying and meaning different things to different groups such as citizens, corporate entities, and governmental regulators. Moreover, in addition to an already complex relationship between environmental justice and policy stakeholders, as well as grass roots organizers and activists, the concept is also defined by the participatory role of advocacy groups.[154] Despite these complexities and differences in interest, the Obama Administration has pressed forward with several initiatives, including those focused on environmental sustainment, by allocating significant fiscal resources to support ecological development.[155]

Communities across the United States are intentionally using renewable energy technology, green infrastructure, recycling, and brownfield redevelopment to create jobs, improve economies, and make communities more attractive places to live and work.[156] Although clearly very popular at the current time, the modern policy focus on ecological sustainment is anything but new. Ecological sustainment and the idea of environmentalism actually originate in the Holy Bible. Indeed, it is present in the *Genesis* creation narrative[157] and continues in *Revelation*.

Although the legal basis of environmental justice began with religious and social activists during the Movement,[158] the theological basis of environmental justice originated with the canonical compilation comprising the Holy Bible's epistles and narratives, with an eschatological focus,[159] all written well before antiquity.[160] As an interdisciplinary look at the connection between law and religion, the focus herein is on the concept of environmental justice from an eschatological perspective.[161] It demonstrates continuity in Judeo-Christian thought, extending from the time John wrote *Revelation* to the current theological influences on President Obama—a president elected at the crossroads of race and religion in America.[162] Specifically, in discussing the environmental justice movement, this discussion argues that *Revelation* delivers a clarion call to all members of Judeo-Christian faith groups to be protective stewards of planet Earth, as they live in joyful anticipation of the time when the triune God will descend to live on Earth as a new Heaven.[163]

Revelation's Message of Hope

Revelation reads like a piece of contemporary pulp fiction.[164] According to New Testament scholar Brian Blount, the president of Union Presbyterian Seminary, John's *Revelation* narrative does not move in a straight line. Instead, *Revelation* begins in the "middle of the story, provides multiple peeks at the arrival of the end of time from unique camera angles (seventh seal, seventh trumpet, seventh bowl), [and] flashes back to the beginning of the story, in the middle of the narrative . . . "[165]

Professor Blount also notes that as *Revelation* shifts to its "wondrous" end in chapters 20 and 21, the approach has already been screened three times in chapters 1 through 6.[166] Further, other scholars of various socio-cultural perspectives view *Revelation* as "unveil[ing] the vision of a world-in-the-making, a vision of justice and peace embodied in a new heaven, . . . earth, and . . . Jerusalem . . . deliver[ing] a . . . challenge for believers to *withdraw from the Empire and to live in . . . service of the God who is making all things new.*[167] Accordingly, notwithstanding *Revelation*'s apocalyptic nature, it bears a message of optimism and hope that springs eternal.[168]

Furthermore, John wrote *Revelation* in the sociopolitical and cultural context of first century Rome. During this period, as evidenced by the re-conquest of Palestine and destruction of Jerusalem at the end of the Jewish revolt, the Roman conquest was at its height. It is from this foundational and sociopolitical understanding of the Roman Empire's imperialism and influence on John's writing of *Revelation* that attention is now directed to the ecological aspect of John's theology of eschatology.

The "Rapture in Reverse" Ecological Message

In transitioning from a general overview to look more specifically at *Revelation* through a lens of ecological eschatology, there is a contrasting vision between Babylon (a code name for Rome) and "New Jerusalem." This offers a perspective on environmentalism and ecological imperialism, in contrast to the promise of a renewed urban world wherein God takes up residence on Earth.[169] John uses the imagery of both cities, Babylon (Rome) and New Jerusalem, to critique Roman dominion during the last decade of the first century, when Domitian was emperor.[170] John's contrasting imagery in *Revelation*, therefore, uses Jewish symbolism in inviting the reader to leave one city to participate in the other.

In further giving *Revelation* an ecological interpretation, as a fundamental starting point, part of the popularly described New Testament rapture theology underscores a common belief that humankind will ascend into the heavens to be with God at the *Parousia*, or second coming of Christ.[171] In *Revelation*, however, John instead describes a "rapture in reverse" whereby God descends to take up residence on Earth.[172] As such, *Revelation* indicates that God loves the Earth and comes to dwell on it.[173] The entire book leads up to John's vision of God's descent to Earth and the renewal of the world.[174]

After chapter 21:2-3, Heaven is not mentioned again in *Revelation,* a striking fact given how central it is in the narrative up to that point. Indeed, "[t]his is because God's throne moves down to [E]arth . . . *Revelation* emphasizes that our future dwelling will be with God on Earth, in a radiant, thriving city landscape. The New Jerusalem comes down out of heaven to Earth, and the home of God will be with his people."[175] In *Revelation,* John writes that "in the spirit, [God] carried [him] away to a great, high mountain and showed . . . the holy city Jerusalem *coming down out of heaven* from God."[176] *Revelation* therefore encourages humans to be wise stewards of the Earth because it provides that God will descend to live with humans, as opposed to humans ascending to live with God in Heaven.[177] This is the very essence of a "rapture in reverse" environmental theology.

An Understanding of "Woes" in *Revelation*

Again, *Revelation*'s organic structure is anything but linear. As Professor Blount argues, its "beginning" is in chapter twelve.[178] In building upon *Revelation*'s rapture in reverse theology and noting chapter twelve's introductory nature, the concept of "woes" should be understood within this biblical context. Terrifying declarations of woe permeate *Revelation*'s middle chapters, causing some to believe the book predicts destruction for the Earth.[179] "Beginning with the fourth trumpet of *Revelation* 8, in the middle of *Exodus*-like plagues, such announcements of "woe" are frequent—and they are cited by rapture proponents and others to argue God consigned Earth to suffer plagues of ecological disaster and ultimate destruction."[180]

In actuality, however, with *Revelation*'s "woes" God is not pronouncing a curse. Instead, God is only offering "a lament, bemoaning [E]arth's conquest and abuse by Roman imperial powers."[181] Additionally, "*Revelation*'s 'woes' must be read in light of the book's overall critique of Rome."[182] Consequently, in linguistically interpreting *Revelation*'s "woes", it should be noted that:

> [T]he Greek word that is usually translated "woe" (*ouai*) is not easy to translate into English. It is a cry or sound in Greek that can be used to express lamentation or mourning...[T]he Greek word *ouai* is better translated consistently as "alas!" or "How awful!" throughout the entire book of *Revelation*. Lamentation or "alas" is clearly the sense of the word *ouai* that is used...[183]

This linguistic distinction is critically important to show that John's theology of eschatology does not suggest God has pronounced a curse but only laments Rome's abuse of Earth's natural resources.[184]

The End of Roman Domination of the Earth

A movement builds upon the traditions of an oppressed people or a group rallying against a dominant power. The environmental justice movement is no different. In *Revelation*, John depicts the end of Roman domination of the Earth by indicating that the time has come for the Earth's destroyers to be destroyed themselves.[185] Thus, according to this critically important verse, God will not destroy the Earth. Instead, in the interest of justice, God will only destroy those that seek to marginalize and objectify others—the very acts of the dominant imperial regime described in *Revelation*. "In the view of *Revelation*, God will not tolerate Rome's destruction of the earth much longer, despite Rome's claim to rule forever. In fact, [*Revelation*'s] so-called end-times language was probably chosen deliberately. . .to counter Rome's imperial and eschatological claims to eternal greatness."[186] This scriptural perspective makes a crucial difference in terms of both an eschatological and ecological understanding of the Bible's last book. *Revelation* is an invitation to join in a movement against marginalization and imperial domination, knowing that justice will indeed prevail.

Elisabeth Schussler Fiorenza, a professor at Harvard Divinity School, argues that much of *Revelation*'s imagery, including Jesus as the Lamb who takes on the role of Moses, originates in *Exodus*.[187] Professor Fiorenza's insight confirms the Judeo-Christian nature of John's *Revelation* narrative, linking together the ancient Hebrew Scriptures with the Christian New Testament's fulfillment of the messianic promise. Indeed, there is a connection and parallelism between the Christians' journey out of Rome and the Israelites' journey out of Egypt.[188]

In writing the *Revelation* narrative, John calls on its readers to "come out" of Babylon, with a connection to Moses and the *Exodus* narrative wherein God's servants sing the song of Moses.[189] In this way, *Revelation* directly connects to its readers with a re-reading of *Exodus* by calling on them to come out of Rome. It is with this understanding that the biblical reader can appreciate the ways in which *Revelation* uses the *Exodus* story and images of plagues as a wake-up call, warning Roman oppressors to repent.[190] There is a direct link between an ecological appreciation of *Revelation* and the ancient Hebrew Scriptures.

As humankind waits for God's throne to descend to Earth, *Revelation* calls for humans to care for the Earth. In post-modernity, biblical readers can appreciate *Revelation*'s ecological message by drawing on the contrast, described by John, demonstrated in its two competing cities.

While Babylon (Rome) represents an ethical critique of environmental oppression, New Jerusalem represents limitless opportunity. Accordingly, the biblical reader is invited to reject oppression and choose opportunity by rejecting Babylon and accepting New Jerusalem. Thus, "the Babylon vision can offer a prophetic critique of environmental injustice and ecological imperialism."[191] This cultural hermeneutic is consistent with liberationist interpretations, including those by womanist, feminist, and Black-liberation theologians.

"*Revelation* 17-18 depicts the Roman Empire as a powerful market economy, a great prostitute that has 'seduced' and 'intoxicated' rulers and nations with its trafficking."[192] Accordingly, as believers await the rapture in reverse, John's *Revelation* narrative invites them to reject environmental *injustice* and embrace environmental justice. This is the very heart that fueled and continues to fuel the ongoing Movement.

The Environmental Movement in Post-Modernity

Alice Kaswan, a noted environmental law and policy scholar and law professor at the University of San Francisco, describes when the environmental justice movement began. Specifically, she describes the 1982 opposition of an African-American community in North Carolina to a potentially hazardous waste landfill being placed within their community and the consequential national exposure that precipitated numerous national studies on the distribution of environmental hazards.[193] As a result of these initial studies, in "1990...the Environmental Protection Agency created the

Environmental Equity Workgroup...to examine the distributional issues raised by environmental policies and enforcement."[194] These significant events laid the foundation for the Clinton Administration, in 1994, to issue "an Executive Order designed to assess and address the demographic issues associated with federal actions and to improve public participation procedures."[195]

The environmental justice movement "[became] multi-issue and multi-racial in scope . . . address[ing] disparities borne by the poor as well as people of color, acknowledging the substantial overlap between the two demographic categories."[196] Indeed, the communities most affected by decisions on environmental regulation were excluded from the decision-making process, either intentionally or because of a lack of resources and structural impediments, including poverty, lack of education, and an inability to participate in the social exchange of information by "others" outside of their communities. Regardless, however, members of those communities engaged in direct action, including protests and demonstrations to bring awareness to their cause.

In an unmistakable manner, therefore, the environmental justice movement's methodologies of direct action and grassroots campaigns in the 1980s and 1990s originated within the larger Movement, dating back to the 1950s and 1960s. Indeed, the same connectedness that existed between the law and theology used by Martin Luther King, Jr. and other members of the clergy to give a voice to the socially marginalized exists in the environmental justice movement's attempt to give a voice to the environmentally marginalized.

As a further testament to the interdisciplinary connectedness between law and religion within the Movement, the United Church of Christ's Commission on Racial Justice (UCC) was intimately involved in the early environmental justice movement, producing a 1987 report—only four years after the United States General Accounting Office's (USGAO) 1983 report—detailing environmental hazards in poor and minority communities. The USGAO's 1983 report found that three of four major offsite hazardous waste facilities were located in predominately African-American communities. The UCC's 1987 report also found a direct correlation between racial minorities and proximity to commercial hazardous waste facilities and uncontrolled waste sites. There was also a follow-up UCC report, published twenty-years after the initial findings were made public, confirming that environmental discrimination indeed exists as an impediment to the quality of life in poor Black communities.[197] The essential public awareness, achieved through direct action demonstrations and white papers, was arguably the first step in achieving distributional justice within the environmental justice movement.

The environmental justice movement is a part of the larger Civil Rights Movement in America. Regardless of whether one assumes that Movement originated with Rosa Parks' act of civil disobedience in 1955, or argues that it was already in motion at least as early as 1954 when the Supreme Court decided *Brown v. Board of Education*, the environmental justice movement is a continuing part of the Movement because, by definition, it requires acts of "civil challenge" to petition the government on behalf of people negatively affected by environmental injustices. Indeed, given the previously described origins of the environmental justice movement, it should come as no surprise that it began in the South, a place with a history of racial issues where marginalized groups were forced to seek governmental redress. Thus, the environmental justice movement's very nature uses the First Amendment to petition the government to remedy injustices.

President Clinton's Executive Order 12,898 (the Order)[198] was the most well known effort to improve the distributional outcomes of environmental decision-making. In relevant part, it required that each federal agency make environmental justice part of its mission by identifying and addressing disproportionately high and adverse environmental effects of the agency's programs, policies, and activities on minority and low-income populations. Moreover, the Order also required federal agencies to develop environmental justice strategies, identifying distributional implications of existing programs, and mandating that federal agencies gather information regarding the demographic consequences of their policy decisions. Indeed, "by explicitly requiring that demographic information be gathered and incorporated into the decision-making process, environmental justice advocates hope[d] the Executive Order would lead to fairer distribution of the consequences of federal agency actions."[199]

In addition to requiring federal agencies to consider demographic effects, the Order also provides that under Title VI of the Civil Rights Act of 1964, "federally funded programs and agencies are prohibited from discriminating on the basis of race, color, or national origin."[200] This proactive governmental perspective with regard to setting environmental justice policy continues under President Obama. Even though governmental agencies have rule-making authority, some legal scholars argue that legislation is still necessary to address environmental justice concerns.[201]

Theology of the Environmental Justice Movement

The basis for humans behaving as wise stewards of the Earth's precious resources is literally as old as time itself. While those in civilized societies have a duty to respect laws, they also have a greater responsibility when self-identifying with Judeo-Christian faith groups. For example, just as someone would not commit murder because of society's penal laws, if the individual is a faith practitioner, their refusal to commit the crime would presumably also be preempted by the Sixth Commandment, a part of the law handed down from Moses well before any post-modern governmental criminal

73

statutes or ordinances were enacted. In much the same regard, just as someone might not pollute the environment because of potential legal consequences, if the person is a member of a Judeo-Christian faith tradition, they should practice wise environmental stewardship because of the calls to do so in *Revelation*. Satisfying this moral and faith-based obligation, centered on environmental justice, is part of accepting the dual keys of legacy and responsibility that were passed on from Jesus to Peter and passed on from those in the original Movement to society at-large today. Indeed, the keys are being passed.

Although *Revelation* has been popularly regarded as a prediction of doom, it should rightfully be viewed as a source of hope. Believers should rejoice in the anticipated second coming as they await the foretold "rapture in reverse." In preparation for God's return, believers are called on to be a part of the environmental justice movement and do today just what John urged in *Revelation*—reject Rome's (the post-modern dominant power structure's) abuse of the Earth and be wise stewards of it in anticipation of the joyful end.

Chapter 6

Environmental Justice and "Letter From Birmingham Jail"

According to the EPA's own reports, the South has more states with environmentally hazardous sites than any other region . . . Texas, Louisiana, Alabama, Florida, and North Carolina are excessively contaminated, and Tennessee, in particular, is one of the most environmentally toxic states in the nation. The South also continues to be the region where most African Americans reside.

- Professor Andrea Simpson[202]

Then I saw a new heaven and a new earth; for the first heaven and the first earth had passed away, and the sea was no more. And I saw the holy city, the new Jerusalem, coming down out of heaven from God, prepared as a bride adorned for her husband. And I heard a loud voice from the throne saying, "See, the home of God is among mortals. He will dwell with them as their God; they will be his peoples, and God himself will be with them; he will wipe out every tear from their eyes..." Then he said to me, "It is done! I am the Alpha and the Omega, the beginning and the end. To the thirsty, I will give water as a gift from the spring of the water of life."

- *Revelation* 21:1-6 (NRSV)

2013 marked the fiftieth anniversary of *Letter From Birmingham Jail*, written by the late Reverend Dr. Martin Luther King, Jr. ("King") after his Good Friday arrest in Birmingham, Alabama, while protesting against what he often called "the iron feet of oppression." In responding to fellow clergy who called King's dissident actions "unwise and untimely," *Letter From Birmingham Jail* was an indictment on the state of injustice in America, especially the Deep South. For King, the clergy's role in the Movement was a response to the legal system's contradiction between ideals of law and justice and the reality of legally sanctioned discrimination against minorities.[203]

Much has changed in the fifty years since King wrote *Letter From Birmingham Jail*. The Movement has continued with, among other things, an ongoing fight for "environmental justice."[204] Arguably, however, the most significant change in America since King wrote *Letter From Birmingham Jail* has been the election of Barack Obama—the United States' first Black president—a president elected at the arguably unprecedented intersection of race and religion in American culture.[205] Indeed, the mere opportunity for Obama to seek the presidency, let alone be elected, was exactly the crux of King's famous 1963 "I Have A Dream" speech.

The Obama Administration has given significant attention to environmental justice, especially as the concept relates to low-income, minority citizens.[206] Furthermore, Obama's environmental policy focus has included job creation that challenges America to become less dependent on the oil and gas industries of the past and move more toward energy-efficient jobs.[207] Most significantly, however, in proverbially "putting his money where his mouth is," the president's green challenge also came with financial support in the form of the American Recovery and Reinvestment Act of 2009 ("ARRA" or "the Stimulus"),[208] which included significant fiscal allocations to states and/or state agencies charged with job training and development.

As part of the environmental justice movement, the Obama Administration's policies have particularly benefited the state of Louisiana in its on-going recovery from the devastation of Hurricane Katrina, as more and more Blacks have the opportunity to live in eco-friendly conditions. In essence, therefore, Louisiana, a southern state with a documented history of racial issues,[209] is setting the benchmark for a "new South" and new environmental justice movement by implementing ecologically-friendly reforms in the wake of devastation and destruction, and by building "green communities"[210] and creating "green jobs."[211] With the assistance of ARRA funds, as well as a ten million dollar National Emergency Grant ("NEG") allocation from the U.S. Department of Labor ("USDOL") to retrain and retool workers for future job industries,[212] Louisiana is leading the South in a new civil rights movement. Indeed, any modern civil rights movement must correlate with economic opportunity for all Americans.

In exploring the intersection between the Movement and the environmental justice movement, within the context of King's sentiments expressed in the *Letter from*

Birmingham Jail it is useful to revisit the context in which he wrote it. As noted by Professor Carlton Waterhouse:

> When King raised issues of moral justice, he drew upon an ideal rooted in the classical western natural law tradition. This tradition, grown from the writings of Greek philosophers and the Christian scholars that influenced many of the sacred texts of Judaism and Christianity, viewed justice as part of the natural order of the universe created by God and comprehended by human beings through their ability to reason. In this tradition, the laws of society are secondary to a higher law that establishes the right and the good.[213]

By April 1963, when King was incarcerated and wrote *Letter From Birmingham Jail*, he was already internationally known for his nonviolent leadership in the 1955 Montgomery Bus Boycott. Moreover, by August 1963, King would receive further international acclaim for his famous "I Have A Dream" speech, given at the culmination of the historic March on Washington.

As a member of the clergy, King accepted a natural leadership role in the Movement's "social gospel"[214] because of his independence in serving a predominately Black congregation. King's views on social justice—presented through sermons, speeches, books, and other writings—are well preserved for future generations, along with biographical narratives.[215] He benefited from an excellent education and an ability to connect with both the

Black masses who suffered from Jim Crow segregation in the South and the Whites in the North who were committed to the ideals of liberalism.[216] Indeed, King's education, ability, and experience—having grown up the son of a prominent Baptist minister—made him a natural leader in the Movement.

Social conditions in 1963 were drastically different from social conditions today. For example, although America has since elected Barack Obama as its first Black president, in 1963, Blacks in many southern states did not yet have the right to vote.[217] Consequently, in protest against what he genuinely believed to be "unjust laws," King often employed direct action and civil disobedience.

Furthermore, from King's theological perspective, human equality stemmed from the identity of *all* humans as being children of God, the very essence of "agape."[218] As Peter Paris, professor emeritus of Princeton Theological Seminary, writes:

> King's vision of the kinship of humans as a direct corollary of the parenthood of God pervaded his entire thought. Only the divine principal of love can hold the diversity of humankind together in a harmonious community. That kinship of persons under the parenthood of God was, in King's mind, the kingdom of God...His fundamental ethical norm was the Christian understanding of love as presented primarily in the Sermon on the Mount and as symbolized most vividly in the cross on which Jesus died while forgiving his enemies.

King viewed Jesus as the
supreme manifestation of that
religious and ethical
principle.[219]

Consequently, in defending the dissident actions that
provoked King's 1963 arrest in Birmingham, and
describing King as one who treated the law with respect,
Professor Paris also wrote:

Martin Luther King's respect
for the law is well known. He
constantly sought to convince
his followers that nonviolent
direct action did not imply any
disrespect for the just laws of
the land, inasmuch as it was
always practiced for the sake
of legal justice. Further, the
method is justified by the
Constitution of the United
States, which provides for
legal protest as a means for
the redress of grievances. King
opposed all forms of anarchy
with a passion similar to that
with which he opposed
tyranny. Since he considered
the fundamental problem in
America to be the moral
cleavage between the national
practice and the law of the
cosmos, and since the civil
rights movement was intended
to be the agent of moral
reform, he advocated a method
for that reform that he could
justify by an appeal to the

moral law of the universe. He
deemed it significant that the
Constitution was a document
that described truths in accord
with that moral law. However,
he viewed the nation's customs
and practices as contradictions
of that law, and consequently,
he   had   no   difficulty   in
appealing to the Constitution
as a source for justifying many
of his actions since that law
was commensurate with the
universal moral law.[220]

Accordingly, one can argue that King's conscious
defiance of unjust laws in 1963 was mandated by his moral
beliefs and practice of evangelical liberalism. Indeed, this
undergirding theology supported the Movement's very
essence.

The Movement's Environmental Legacy

The general consensus of scholarship regards the
environmental justice movement's origins as an outgrowth
of the larger Civil Rights Movement in America.[221] Some
argue the environmental justice movement was formed
through diversity of organizing efforts, which included
Native Americans, labor, and to a lesser extent, the
traditional environmental movement.[222] Indeed, the
environmental justice literature cites an African-American
community's 1982 opposition to a toxic landfill in Warren
County,   North   Carolina,   as   the   genesis   of   the
environmental justice movement.[223]

As a result of the Warren County community's
opposition and the initial 1982 studies detailing
environmental hazards in communities of color, the USGO
issued its 1983 report, followed by the UCC's 1987 study

that "found a positive correlation between racial minorities and proximity to commercial hazardous waste facilities and uncontrolled waste sites."[224] Consequently, by "1990, the federal government weighed in when the Environmental Protection Agency created the Environmental Equity Workgroup...to examine the distributional issues raised by environmental policies and enforcement."[225]

As a basis of organizing, the First National People of Color Environmental Leadership Summit was held in Washington, D.C., October 24–27, 1992.[226] The Summit's results included adoption of a declaration called the *Principles of Environmental Justice.* In relevant part, the declaration proclaims:

> WE THE PEOPLE OF COLOR, gathered together at this multinational *People of Color Environmental Leadership Summit,* to build a national and international movement of all peoples of color to fight the destruction and takings of our lands and communities, do hereby re-establish our spiritual interdependence to the sacredness of our Mother Earth; to respect and celebrate each of our cultures, languages and beliefs about the natural world and our roles in healing ourselves; to ensure environmental justice; to promote economic alternatives that would contribute to the development of environmentally safe livelihoods; and, to secure our political, economic and cultural liberation that has been denied for over 500 years of colonization and oppression, resulting in the positioning of our communities and land and the

genocide of our peoples, to affirm and adopt these Principles of Environmental Justice:

1. Environmental justice affirms the sacredness of Mother Earth, ecological unity and interdependence of all species, and the right to be free from ecological destruction.
2. Environmental justice demands that public policy be based on mutual respect and justice for all peoples, free from any form of discrimination or bias.
3. Environmental justice mandates the right to ethical, balanced and responsible uses of land and renewable resources in the interest of a sustainable planet for humans and other living things.
. . .
5. Environmental justice affirms the fundamental right to political, economic, cultural, and economic determination of all peoples.
. . .
7. Environmental justice demands the right to participate as equal partners at every level of decision-making including needs assessment, planning, implementation, enforcement and evaluation.
. . .
14. Environmental justice opposes the destructive operations of multinational corporations.
. . .
17. Environmental justice requires that we, as individuals, make personal and consumer choices to consume as

little of Mother Earth's resources and
to produce as little waste as possible;
and make the conscious decision to
challenge and reprioritize our lifestyles
to insure the health of the natural
world for present and future
generations.[227]

The success of this grass roots activism proved to be a
basis for federal intervention in years to come.

The foregoing events set a foundation for the Clinton
Administration, in 1994, to issue the Order to address the
demographic issues associated with federal actions and
improve public participation procedures.[228] The essential
public awareness achieved through direct action
demonstrations and white papers were arguably the first
steps in achieving distributional justice within the
environmental justice movement. Indeed, the Order was
arguably the "most well-known effort to improve the
distributional outcomes of environmental decision
making."

Furthermore, the Order also requires federal agencies
to develop environmental justice strategies, identifying
distributional implications of existing programs, and
mandating that federal agencies gather information
regarding demographic consequences of their policy
decisions.[229] Consequently, "[b]y explicitly requiring that
demographic information be gathered and incorporated
into decision-making sic] processes, environmental justice
advocates hope[d] the. . .Order [would] lead to a fairer
distribution of the consequences of federal agency
actions."[230] This pro-active governmental perspective on
setting environmental justice policy began with the Order
in the Clinton Administration and clearly continues under
President Obama.

This emphasis on creating paths to achieving
environmental justice in America is an important step
down the road to accomplishing the ultimate goals of the

environmental justice movement. Achieving this justice is critical to the lives of millions of Americans. It is important because in the absence of such environmental justice lives are impacted negatively, and not only this, but lives are being lost due to the current state of environmental injustice in America. One glaring example of this is what Hurricane Katrina revealed when it came ashore. As the Institute for Women's Policy Research wrote:

> The entire country watched in shock as Hurricanes Katrina and Rita hit the Gulf Coast, bringing flooding and devastation to the region. The devastation to many victims' lives, however, was caused by more than physical damage brought on by the hurricanes...The hurricanes uncovered America's longstanding structural inequalities based on race, gender, and class and laid bare the consequences of ignoring these underlying inequalities.[231]

The U.S. Congress estimates that in the wake of a delayed evacuation order for the city of New Orleans, more than 70,000 residents remained in the city to be rescued after Hurricane Katrina.[232] The storm's catastrophic nature brought into high relief many of the social and socioeconomic inequities that remained vestiges in New Orleans after the 1960s. As Loyola University New Orleans law professor Bill Quigley writes, "disasters rip off our social bandages and lay bare long-neglected injustices, providing a new lens to view the real lives and living conditions of our sisters and brothers."[233] Further, one need look only to the areas of the city that have been revived and thriving in comparison with the areas of the city that still have not been rebuilt post-Katrina, to see environmental injustice still at play in New Orleans.

Environmental Justice and Theology Today

If King were alive today, would he recognize the current South in contrast to the way things were in 1963? Would King believe the tactics that he used in 1963 would be equally as successful for the environmental justice movement in the 1980s and beyond? Indeed, as an ordained minister who was obviously committed to incorporating religious beliefs into a social gospel, one could logically conclude that if King were alive today, his environmentalism would be theologically oriented and expressed.[234]

In reading *Revelation* through a lens of ecological eschatology,[235] there exists a contrasting vision between Babylon (a code name for "Rome") and a "new" Jerusalem. The portrayed difference offers a prophetic critique of environmentalism and ecological imperialism, in contrast to the promise of a renewed urban world wherein God takes up residence on Earth.[236] John, the presumed author of *Revelation*, uses the imagery of both cities, Babylon and "new" Jerusalem, to critique Roman dominion during the last decade of the first century, when Domitian was emperor.[237] John's contrasting imagery in *Revelation* deploys Jewish symbolism as a way of inviting the reader to leave one city to journey through the other. From a theological perspective, therefore, if King were alive today, he might agree with the argument that humans have a moral duty to serve as good stewards of the Earth as they await God's return to it.[238]

Part of the popularly described New Testament rapture theology underscores a common belief that humankind will ascend into the heavens to be with God at the second coming of Christ. In *Revelation*, however, there instead is a "rapture in reverse" whereby God descends to take up residence on Earth.[239] As such, *Revelation* indicates God loves the Earth and will come to dwell in it.[240]

If King were alive today, he might be influenced by environmental scholars like John Dernbach, a lay preacher in the Episcopal Church and distinguished law professor at Widener University, who advocates an ecological reading of the Holy Bible. On Earth Day in 2001,[241] Professor Dernbach preached at the Cathedral Church of St. Stephens in Harrisburg, Pennsylvania. He emphasized the connection between the planet God gave humanity and humanity's obligation to be a prudent trustee of God's gift.

In preaching about Saint Mark's portrayal of the story in *Saint Mark*, 12:28-31, in which Jesus says there are two great commandments, Professor Dernbach notes that when one of the scribes asked Jesus which commandment was first of all, Jesus answered by proclaiming:

> The first is "Hear, O Israel: the Lord our God, the Lord is one; you shall love the Lord with all your heart, and with all your soul, and with all your mind, and with all your strength." The second is this, "You shall love your neighbor as yourself." There is no other commandment greater than these.

According to Professor Dernbach, the ecological exegesis of Jesus' response finds its origins in the Old Testament's *Genesis* 1:28. As such, having "dominion"[242] over the Earth has an associated responsibility of loving the Earth's resources because they are shared with one's neighbors.

If King were alive today, he likely would not recognize the "new South." Indeed, if he were alive, he would probably join in the new South's continuing environmental justice movement. King's theological training, as a minister of the social gospel, suggests his likely ecological advocacy would be theologically based. King would therefore likely agree with Professor Dernbach in encouraging humanity to live as prudent stewards of the Earth while waiting in joyful anticipation of God's descent to dwell on it. In choosing a place to live, perhaps King might move to New Orleans—the arguable capitol of the new South and an obvious leader in a new environmental justice movement. Indeed, the South has come a long way in the fifty years since he wrote *Letter From Birmingham Jail.*

Chapter 7

You Have Power

**(A Sermon Preached at Dillard University's
Lawless Memorial Chapel)**

*In the first book, Theophilus, I
wrote about all that Jesus did
and taught from the beginning
until the day when he was
taken up to heaven, after
giving instructions through the
Holy Spirit to the apostles
whom he had chosen. After his
suffering he presented himself
alive to them by many
convincing proofs, appearing to
them during forty days and
speaking about the kingdom of
God. While staying with them,
he ordered them not to leave
Jerusalem, but to wait there
for the promise of the Father.
"This," he said, "is what you
have heard from me; for John
baptized with water, but you
will be baptized with the Holy
Spirit not many days from
now."*

*So when they had come
together, they asked him,
"Lord, is this the time when
you will restore the kingdom of
to Israel?" He replied, "It is not
for you to know the times or
periods that the Father has set*

89

> *by his own authority. But you
> will receive power when the
> Holy Spirit has come upon you;
> and you will be my witnesses
> in Jerusalem, in Judea and
> Samaria, and to the ends of
> the earth."*

- *The Book of Acts* 1:1-8 (NRSV)

My older brother recently moved back to Louisiana, after having spent his entire adult life living in California. In moving back, like anyone else, he had some adjustments in relearning his former surroundings. One afternoon, we were out in my car and he told me he had a taste for some catfish. I LOVE catfish! I reached in my pocket and pulled out my phone and said "Siri, where's the nearest catfish restaurant?" He looked at me and said, "Hey man, who is that?" I told him Siri is my personal assistant that comes with the iPhone system. He said he needed a Siri to help get him around, too. So, I took him to the AT&T store to get an iPhone after, of course, we ate our catfish.

The sales representative pulled the phone out and gave him an overview of all the iPhone's features. He was amazed to learn of all the things it could do. His only concern, as the red warning light came on in the store, was whether he'd be able to do all those things once he got the phone home. The sales associated assured him he would be able to do all those things, and more. He just had to plug it up because it needed to revive its energy source. Simply put, it needed power. In other words, to reach full capacity the phone couldn't exist on its own. It needed something to fuel its fire. What I'm trying to say is that it needed power!

In talking with you for just a few moments this morning on the topic "You Have Power," I want to be clear in defining the type of power I'm talking about. By way of contrast, let me give you two examples of what I'm not talking about. I'm not talking about what I call the "Power of Position" that comes along with a person's authority. Let me give you an example. When I graduated from the Army ROTC program in college, at probably 22-years of age, I was commissioned as a lieutenant in the United States Army. By virtue of my position as an officer, when I walked into a room, grown men, as I called them, would stop, stand-up, and say "Group, Attention!" That power had nothing to do with me as a person. It only had to do with my position in the hierarchy of the United States military and it had a lot to do with a fear of what might happen if someone didn't stand-up when the lieutenant walked into the room. That's "Power of Position."

There is also what I call the "Power of Trust." It comes about after people get to know and respect you and place confidence in what you say, such that they will seek your advice on matters that may be of very personal importance. For example, when as a pastor I sit and talk with someone who says: "Reverend, I'm having a problem with my daughter" or "there's a serious issue with my son," or "I'm thinking about leaving my spouse," they inevitably will end the explanation with the question, "What do you think I should do?" The confidence those individuals have is an earned confidence that is engendered by their relationship with the person from whom they are seeking advice. I call that sort of power, the "Power of Trust."

To be clear, though, this morning we're not talking about an "Earthly power." We're NOT talking about the "Power of a Position" and we're NOT talking about the "Power of Trust." Instead, we're talking about the "Power of the Holy Spirit." We're talking about the kind of power— like the old timers used to say, "this world didn't give it to you and this world can't take it away." The power we're talking about this morning is not an exclusive power that's only given to an army officer or a pastor. The kind of power we're talking about is the *inclusive* power that's given to those who believe in the original power source, the one who sits up high but also looks down low. What I'm trying to say, my brothers and sisters, is that if you will put yourself in the place of those that believed in power in Jerusalem,

91

you too will receive power, right here at Dillard University in New Orleans. "You Have Power."

I want to take you on what I call a call a "loop" this morning. In doing so, and looking at today's text, I want to talk about: (1) the transition in the text; (2) the transition in our world; (3) God's grace and God's movement in the text; and (4) God's grace and God's movement in our world. If we do this thing right, we will begin Religious Emphasis Week with the full recognition that "You Have Power!"

Before we talk about today's text, I think it's important to lay a foundation for the text. I always say that a biblical text doesn't just appear in a vacuum. Instead, the text is part of the larger story of revelation. Not the *Book of Revelation*—the text is part of how God reveals God's self to humanity. As a Trinitarian Christian, I believe God revealed God's self to humanity as "God the Father" in the Old Testament. I also believe God revealed God's self to humanity in the form of "God the Son" in the four New Testament gospel narratives where we meet the person called Jesus. Here, however, *after* the gospels, in the *Book of Acts*, the second volume of a two volume set written by the author of the *Gospel of Luke*, we see God revealing God's self to humanity in the form of the Holy Spirit. That's the part of the Godhead we met in Jerusalem on the Day of Pentecost and that's the part that remains with all believers forever. What I'm trying to say is that, if you and I are like an iPhone and we have to plug in to get power to function, we must plug into the Holy Spirit, the source of *all* our power.

When we look at the text, we see a certain transition going on with Jesus' disciples. Remember, the text doesn't appear in a vacuum. This part of the story began when Jesus was brutally crucified by order of the Roman authorities and the Jewish Sanhedrin who wanted to put an end to that "trouble maker" named Jesus so they could "keep on keepin' on." They didn't want change! They wanted it like we say here in New Orleans, "red beans and rice on Monday and catfish and gumbo on Friday, baby! We don't want change, no!"

When we look at the text, however, change came. Change came because the person that was crucified on Good Friday arose from the dead on Easter Sunday. Change came because that same person walked the earth again for forty days and made six post resurrection appearances to ensure people knew he was back and that God was indeed still on the throne. Now, at the end of those 40-days, our text is the physician Luke's account of what took place on what we call the Day of the Holy Ascension, as Jesus was going up into heaven.

In the various gospels we have what's called "the Great Commission" where Jesus commands his disciples to go forward and baptize all nations, teaching them as they have been taught. That's a transition of God the Son giving power to the people. Today's text follows Jesus' commission in that it says to us, anytime you're trying to do some good; trouble is going to come. Anytime you're trying to do something different, trouble is going to try and knock you back into the same old, same old. Today's text, therefore, is Jesus giving us the power we need to carry out the Great Commission—he's preparing us to receive the Holy Spirit as the source of *all* our power.

What I'm trying to say is that, somebody here is the first one in their family to go to college and their money might be funny. What we're talking about though, is no laughing matter because "You Have Power." Somebody here made a mistake and now feels as though they are in a dark tunnel and they just don't know if they have it in themselves to make a way out of no way and get out of the tunnel without ruining their life. Listen to me, now: I'm not telling you what I think I know; I'm telling you what I know, I know—"You Have Power." Somebody here may feel lost and not believe God is listening to them—they feel like their iPhone just won't work. I got news for you: Jesus never said life would be easy. Jesus did, however, give us *all* the tools we need to get through the rough parts. That's the beauty of the text. Power isn't just for people in certain positions. The text shows that Jesus is giving us the opportunity to plug into the power source. So, whatever you're going through, the text is telling us just tap into the power source. Jesus gives it to us all. Remember, my brothers and sisters: "You Have Power!"

In addition to looking at the transition in the biblical text, I also want to take a moment to look at transition in our lives. As we celebrate Religious Emphasis Week here at Dillard and tap into the power of the Holy Spirit, we must also be mindful of the fact that we are in the midst of a month-long celebration of Black History. For me February and Black History Month are not so much about a separatism of exclusion, but more so about a diversity of inclusion.

As a person of deep religious conviction, I honor those who helped to transition America in overcoming obstacles by tapping into the power of the Holy Spirit. In other words, those that we honor during this 50-year anniversary celebration of the Civil Rights Movement, we salute for helping transition the United States from the era of Jim Crow to the age of Obama, with an emphasis on inclusion and opportunity, more so than isolation and separation.

To put it in the words of our departed sister from Mississippi, Fannie Lou Hammer, as she said 50-years ago, demanding inclusion so Blacks from the Mississippi Democratic Freedom Party could be seated as delegates at the 1964 Democratic National Convention:

> "We're in this bag together! It doesn't matter if you have a PhD, or a No D! We're in this bag together! It doesn't matter if you went to Morehouse, or you got no house! We're in this bag together!"

As we kick-off Religious Emphasis Week and find ourselves at the intersection of Religious Emphasis and Black History, we must be mindful of the fact that so many of our heroes that literally transitioned the United States of America did so by tapping into the power of their faith by realizing that transition was only possible through acting on faith. What I'm trying to say is that we can't simply talk about Rosa Parks being tired and refusing to give up her seat in the "White section" of a municipal bus without talking about the deeply religious Rosa Parks that tapped into the power of the Holy Spirit as an active member of the steward board at St. Paul AME Church in Montgomery, Alabama. That's power.

We can't simply talk about college students at Fisk in Nashville who boarded Greyhound Buses headed to New Orleans in the Freedom Rides or talk about college students at North Carolina A&T in Greensboro who sat-in at lunch counters without talking about the fact that these students believed in the "Suffering Servant" found in *Isaiah* 53. Those young college students were willing to put their personal safety and even their lives at issue because they were more concerned about solving the problems of segregation and discrimination in public accommodation than they were about temporal convenience. That's power. They couldn't have done those things if they didn't tap into the power of the Holy Spirit. In other words, "They Had Power."

You can't talk about where religious emphasis and civil rights meet without talking about a Baptist preacher from Atlanta, Georgia. You can't talk about a Civil Rights Act of 1964 or a Voting Rights Act of 1965 without talking about how that preacher got down on his knees and tapped into the source of all power when he fought some seriously uphill battles. In recognizing that his power came from up high and *not* here on earth, some say that preacher from Atlanta preached his own eulogy when he acknowledged he wouldn't be around too much longer. He said:

"When you get someone to speak at my funeral, tell them not to talk too long. Tell them don't mention that I have a Nobel Peace Prize . . . That's not important. Tell them don't mention the fact that I have two to three hundred other awards. Tell them don't mention where I went to school. Instead, tell them to simply say that Martin Luther King, Jr. tried to love somebody."

That love that Martin Luther King, Jr. spoke about is a love that's derived from above, *not* here on earth. It's a love that comes from the original power source, the same source of power that's available to all of us here in Lawless Chapel. The source hasn't changed. What I'm trying to say is that "We *ALL* Have Power!"

When we look back at the text, we see the movement of God the almighty because God is making a way for us all. When Jesus is talking to the disciples, notice that he's setting them up for success. He's not saying trouble won't come your way if you follow me. Instead, he's saying I know for a fact that trouble *will* come your way. I also know that if you simply plug into the power source, no matter what issues you have you can overcome all obstacles. That's power!

Notice that in the text Jesus doesn't just say, "Go and be disciples by carrying out the Great Commission...You're ready!" No. No. Instead, Jesus is saying, "Hold just one second, because in order to get through the storm that's waiting for you ahead, you're going to need something to make sure you're successful. You're going to need POWER!" In other words: POWER to get the financial aid you might need for the semester;

POWER to figure out how you're going to pay for your car note; POWER to stay up late and study hard in the class you hate the most...Again, I'm not telling you what I think I know...I'm telling you what I know I know. In order to get past those temporary issues and realize that no matter how big they may seem as you're going through them, you will indeed get through them, just like Rosa Parks got through them. Just like Fannie Lou Hammer got through them. Just like Martin Luther King, Jr. got through them. They all tapped into the power source. That's God's grace in the text. We all can tap into the power source of prayer at any time. We can all tap into the power source of faith. Just tap on in and believe that "You Have Power!"

Just as Jesus gave each of us power in the biblical text, God has also manifested the results of that power in our lives. It's right and it's appropriate to celebrate the legacy of Black History that has already been written. Today, however, as we begin Religious Emphasis Week, I think it's equally important to note that the "Power of God" and the "Power of Prayer" continue to manifest themselves each and every day as we continue to write Black history. The best part about writing Black History now is that the author of this chapter in the book won't be Fannie Lou Hammer or Martin Luther King, Jr. The author of this chapter can't be Zora Neal Hurston or Gwendolyn Brooks. It can't be Phyllis Wheatley or Mary McCloud Bethune and it won't be Alex Haley or John Hope Franklin. The author of this chapter of the book is the person who has the ability to plug in and get *all* the power in the world. It's the person that can pull out pen and paper to write or, more with the times, type it up on an iPad. The author of this chapter is you. What I'm trying to say is that "You have power!"

You are writing a new chapter, my brothers and sisters, but you're building on a legacy that already exists. There's no need to reinvent the wheel. Just use the power of prayer like those before you. You have power because the power of prayer has been passed on to you. That's where Religious Emphasis Week and Black History Month meet. They meet at the "Power of Prayer" and the "Power of the Holy Spirit" because "We All Have Power!"

The legacy of power that manifested in the Movement is again manifesting right here before you're very eyes because the power source has remained the same. If you could plug in the power of prayer and talk to Samuel DeWitt Proctor, I bet he would tell you that "We All Have Power!" I bet if we could plug into the power of prayer and talk with Madame C.J. Walker, Barbara Jordan, or Adam Clayton Powell, Jr., they would all tell us "We All Have Power!" I bet if we could tap into the power of prayer and talk to Ida B. Wells Barnett, Whitney Young, or Medgar W. Evers, they would all tell us "We All Have Power!"

That's the legacy of prayer. That's the power or prayer. It's being passed on to you. "We All Have Power." All you have to do is unlock it by plugging in, too. You have the power of prayer. It's the power God gave to each of us. You don't have to be in the Army. You don't have to be a preacher. "We All Have Power." It's the power of God. I have power. You Have Power. "We All Have Power!"

PART THREE

Leveling the Playing Field:
The Ongoing Fight for Education Reform

Chapter 8

Education Reform as Part of the Civil Rights Movement: The Interest Convergence 2.0

The civil rights movement, like the Reconstruction governments, sought to overturn a deep-seated system of racial subordination, and as it had during Reconstruction, schooling would figure prominently in the struggle. Of particular importance were the Mississippi freedom schools of 1964. In these schools, civil rights workers...worked with volunteers to set up an alternative school system. The summer volunteers, many white and from elite northern universities, tried to educate Mississippi blacks about history, civics, politics, and the means by which they could change society. Beyond the freedom schools' well known contribution to the racial justice struggle, I would suggest that they are important in another, less often recognized way. Just as blacks during Reconstruction refused to accept the absence of schools, the freedom schools movement refused to accept the inadequacy of schools. By building separate schools and openly repudiating the establishment system, the freedom schools movement laid a foundation for later progressive school choice proposals.

- James Foreman, Jr., Yale Law Professor, Co-Founder of Maya Angelou Charter School, Washington, D.C.[243]

In *Brown v. Board of Education*, the United States Supreme Court placed access to educational opportunities at the heart of the Movement. Moreover, in *Grutter v. Bollinger*, decided almost fifty years later, the Court affirmed this position.[244] As a successor to several other reform-oriented enactments, including the Elementary and Secondary Education Act of 1965,[245] the No Child Left Behind Act of 2001 ("NCLB")[246] placed closing the achievement gap between Black and White students at the pinnacle of the ongoing Movement. Indeed, the administration of Democratic President Barack Obama continues the Movement with emphasis on improving education, as exemplified by the Race to the Top (RTT) initiative and the millions of dollars allocated to innovative education reform as part of the Stimulus Package. The Obama administration's reforms are non-partisan. Indeed, they build on the efforts of his Republican predecessor, George W. Bush.[247]

In a time of such pronounced partisanship, the question must be "why?" Why is it, with all the political differences between Presidents Bush and Obama, their stances on the issue of education reform are consistent?[248] Accepting the premise that education reform is part of the ongoing Movement, in a time in which civil rights must also mean economic opportunity, the United States' two major political parties embrace education reform as a pathway to economic development in communities that historically have lacked such opportunities. Moreover, Blacks, who significantly populate America's public schools—especially in urban areas—have a deep interest in education reform, too. The intersection of where those interests meet is what and/or where the late Professor Derrick Bell called the "interest convergence."[249] After *Brown v. Board*'s twenty-fifth anniversary, Professor Bell wrote of the interest convergence leading to *Brown*. In summary, he analyzed why the *Brown* Court moved away from "separate but equal":

101

[T]he decision in *Brown* to break with the Court's long-held position on these issues cannot be understood without some consideration of the decision's value to [W]hites, not simply those concerned about the immorality of racial inequality, but also those [W]hites in policy-making positions able to see the economic and political advances at home and abroad that would follow abandonment of segregation. First, the decision helped to provide immediate credibility to America's struggle with Communist countries to win the hearts and minds of emerging third world peoples...

Second, *Brown* offered much needed reassurance to American [B]lacks that the precepts of equality and freedom so heralded during World War II might yet be given meaning at home. Returning [B]lack veterans faced not only continuing discrimination, but also violent attacks in the South which rivaled those that took place at the conclusion of World War I...

Finally, there were [W]hites who realized that the South could make the transition from a rural, plantation society to the sunbelt with all its potential and profit only when it ended its struggle to remain divided by state-sponsored segregation. Thus, segregation was viewed as a barrier to further industrialization in the South...[250]

In summary, understanding Blacks wanted the best opportunities for educational advancement; their interest converged with Whites, who- notwithstanding goodwill and progressive thinking- wanted economic development.[251] Accordingly, as the groups' interests "converged," *de jure* segregation ended. In essence, therefore, education reform's contemporary focus is the interest convergence theory 2.0. Consequently, contemporary groups like the Black Alliance for Educational Options (BAEO), a national non-profit education reform group, were formed "to increase access to high-quality educational options for Black children by actively supporting parental choice policies and programs that empower low-income and working-class Black families."[252]

In giving the interest convergence theory contemporary application—moving past race and into economics, as part of the on-going Movement, notwithstanding President Obama's reform efforts for *all* students, and the Black community's desire for improved outcomes, some argue Obama's reforms are destroying his Democratic Party by failing to consider ancillary effects on teachers' unions. I specifically refute such criticism. But President Obama's education reform agenda should not be a surprise, based on what then-Senator Obama promised as a candidate for the presidency.[253]

Flawed Criticisms of Race to the Top

Some activists and academics clearly take issue with the Obama Administration's RTT and its incentive-based financial reward for innovation,[254] and America's pro-charter school movement.[255] Although such arguments are premised on the alleged destruction of teacher unions, the American Federation of Teachers' education reform partnership with the Bill and Melinda Gates Foundation (the Gates Foundation) belies any such arguments because such an oversimplification is flawed in at least three regards.[256]

First, any such argument inherently categorizes a political tension between the political "left" and political "right." In actuality, however, the tension is between the "old" and "new" unionism, with the education reform movement now including the voices of change-agents like StudentsFirst, Teach for America and City Year. Democrats have not abandoned teachers or unions. Instead, they respond to ongoing problems with educational outcomes by reimagining what teacher unions can and should be. Additionally, any such argument assumes there are two sides, Republicans and Democrats, with Democrats moving to join Republicans. A more objective analysis shows political unity and a collective desire to improve educational outcomes. Indeed, this was evident by the overwhelming majority of the members of Congress joining together to pass NCLB in 2001.

Second, criticisms of the Obama education reform initiatives as destroying American teacher unions assumes unions are monolithic, when they actually have diverse perspectives on education reform.[257] Finally, any criticism of the Gates Foundation is misguided. Indeed, as a non-partisan stakeholder, the Gates Foundation *works with teachers*, something unions value, in improving educational outcomes.

The policy-oriented goals behind RTT's incentivizing classroom improvements are not new. They date back to *Sputnik*.[258] In the wake of World War II and the Cold War's intensification, concerns arose as to whether the United States could keep up with the Soviet Union in math and science after the 1957 launch of the Soviet Union's space satellite *Sputnik*. Consequently, policymakers pressured public schools to quantify educational improvement to ensure America would not lose the space race. Congress then passed the ESEA in 1965.

ESEA's signature item was Title I, the federal government's largest education aid program.[259] John Jackson, a former White House education policy advisor and president of the Schott Foundation for Public

Education, describes ESEA as providing a clear federal role for education after *Brown* and the Civil Rights Act of 1964, placing America on a course toward sustaining its position as a global leader of opportunity and democracy.[260] Moreover, Damon Hewitt, the director of the NAACP Legal Defense Fund's Education Practice Group, describes ESEA as a civil rights statute designed to level the playing field by expanding opportunity for poor children and children of color.[261]

In the decades following ESEA's enactment, Congress continually poured hundreds of billions of dollars into public education, with lackluster results. Consequently, policy makers must demand systemic change and outcomes-based improvement, something Obama and the progressive left are doing. Indeed, notwithstanding RTT's detractors, RTT receives praise "for inspiring education reforms without dictating the details and without spending a great deal of the money...[Moreover,] [m]any also applaud the priorities of the program, especially its desire to measure teacher performance through student test scores and its encouragement of national standards."[262]

As Congress continually funds education, given the historical return on investment, RTT incentivizes states to break bureaucracy and make much needed reforms.

> Fundamental to the philosophical force behind RTT is the belief... that...competition by the states for such large grant monies will not only engender positive educational steps...but that all states will move toward more constructive educational approaches...*In other words, it is not the money by itself that will produce effective educational reform, but the innovative abilities unleashed by competition.*[263]

The Role of Charter Schools in Educational Reform

Charter schools are vehicles to manifest educational reforms that the RTT seeks to foster. Charter schools are publically financed schools that are open to any child. They differ from "traditional" public schools, however, because they are run by entities other than the conventional school district, typically nonprofit organizations that rely on donations for seed money to launch the school. Once launched, they typically use the same amount, or less, of taxpayer money per pupil for the education of each student. The main difference between charters and traditional public schools is that charters have the autonomy to manage their affairs as they wish, including the autonomy to hire and fire teachers who are not union members.

Although some detractors argue data doesn't support the conclusion charter schools are better than traditional schools, in actuality, anecdotal evidence shows charter schools *are working* in improving results-based outcomes.[264] Moreover, because charter schools often enroll poor children with historic challenges, empirical data has not accumulated to the point that it can be used to irrefutably rebut detractors. Research results suggest, however, that ongoing school reform could significantly reduce racial earning gaps.[265]

As stated by Marian Wright Edelman, head of the Children's Defense Fund:

> So many poor babies...enter the world with multiple strikes already against them...Lack of access to health and mental health care...lack of quality early childhood education to get ready for school; educational disadvantages resulting from failing schools that don't expect to help them achieve or detect and correct early problems that

> impede learning...too few positive
> alternatives to the streets after school
> and in summer months; and too few
> positive role models and mentors in
> their homes . . .[266]

Case studies show the direct correlation between social capital (familial relationships, *etc.*) and educational opportunities.[267] Moreover, regarding race, considerable differences in income earning directly relate to the absence or presence of such opportunities. It is therefore logical that where many "vulnerable students" lack social capital, they simultaneously lack meaningful opportunity to improve their economic status. While White interest in school reform may be in improved learning outcomes through diversity, Black interest is in increased income earning potential. As part of an ongoing Movement, these interests have converged for a paradigm shift: the interest convergence theory 2.0. President Obama recognized this shift when he provided the following statement:

> I want for all children to go to
> schools worthy of their potential-
> schools that challenge them,
> inspire them, and instill in them a
> sense of wonder about the world
> around them. I want them to have
> the chance to go to college- even if
> their parents aren't rich. And I
> want them to get good jobs: jobs
> that pay well and give them
> benefits...[268]

Since education reform began in the wake of *Sputnik*, it has not been immune to controversy. Regardless of partisan perspective, however, America is unified behind the idea that education is the foundation of good citizenship. Indeed, education has also long been regarded as the key to economic opportunity.

Although NCLB was passed as overwhelmingly bipartisan legislation aimed at closing the achievement gap and consequently creating economic opportunity, reaction to Congress' creation of RTT, an incentive-based method to achieve NCLB's goals, has been less sanguine. While RTT is far from perfect, the AFT—a teachers' union that would presumably be opposed to its reforms—has partnered with states in attempting to secure RTT funds.[269] Moreover, the AFT also supports new standards for teacher evaluation and pay as well as charter schools. In *Brown*, ethnic interests converged to end segregation. In current reform, economic interests converge to improve education. In this sense, accepting the dual keys of legacy and responsibility mean supporting and promoting a return to the autonomous nature of individual educational institutions with an accountability model that demands results for Black and other underprivileged children.

Chapter 9

Leaving No Child Behind Means
Establishing Equality in Public Education

Because of the public
perception that schools hold
the major obligation for
educating children, schools
tend to get the lion's share of
the blame for the achievement
gap. It is not surprising then
that when the nation looks to
ways to reduce or close the gap,
the major attention tends to be
aimed at improving schools.
Recent research has yielded a
much clearer understanding of
the extent to which and the
ways in which school variables
influence the achievement gap.
The belief that good schools
have a powerful impact on
student achievement was the
driving force behind the No
Child Left Behind (NCLB) Act.
In 2001, for the first time in
our nation's history, closing the
Black-White achievement gap
was determined to be of such
importance to our national
interest that it became a matter
of federal policy. The purpose
of the bill was clearly stated
right up front on the title page:
'To close the achievement gap
with accountability, flexibility,

and choice, so that no child is left behind.[270]

As part of the 50th Anniversary of the Movement's 1964 legislative achievements, education reform advocates can also celebrate and recall the significance of the Johnson Administration's support for, and Congress' passage of the Elementary and Secondary Education Act of 1965 ("ESEA").[271] In 2001, as a bipartisan means of bringing about significant substantive change in public education, Congress acted to pass ESEA's most recent incarnation, the No Child Left Behind Act of 2001 ("NCLB").[272] NCLB was Republican President George W. Bush's signature education reform legislation.

One of NCLB's most significant reform measures was to create "choice,"[273] thus allowing children attending "failed" or "failing" public schools to transfer to other public schools that meet accountability benchmark standards. The purpose of choice was obviously to ensure that children would have the opportunity to receive a quality education. Many presumed NCLB would level the inherently unequal playing field that was the subject of *Brown v. Board of Education* and hundreds of other educational inequality cases that resulted from the *Brown* Court's ruling. As a matter of practical application, however, recent years have proven true the old cliché– "Hindsight is always 20/20." Considering NCLB through the 20/20 lens of hindsight, it is obvious that the law has significant ancillary effects and arguably doesn't do far enough in improving educational outcomes for Black children.

Assuming a student exercises NCLB's choice provision and transfers to a school that meets its academic benchmarks, the rhetorical question becomes, "[w]hat happens to the failing school from which the student transferred?" The practical reality is that in many states, charter schools have proliferated and assumed control of "failed" public schools, allowing for on-going experimentation with educational reform measures.

In analyzing the practical effects of NCLB's theoretical solutions addressing the problem of racial inequality in public education, Louisiana's public education system serves as a good real-world model for the law's application. I support a tripartite partnership approach to educating public school children with a synergy between: (1) the local school district and/or individual school, (2) the local community, particularly faith-based and business organizations, and (3) the students, parents, guardians or primary caretakers.

The tripartite partnership is the best model for maximizing stakeholder involvement, and in a state like Louisiana, where charter schools appear to be at the center of a nationally observed experiment, it is arguably the only model that will lead to sustained success in achieving the clear and unequivocal aim of NCLB: closing the achievement gap. In order to reform public education as part of the on-going Movement and close the achievement gap, there must be a synergistic relationship between the: (1) local school district and individual school; (2) students and parents, guardians or primary caretakers; and (3) local faith-based and business organizations. Making the proposed changes to NCLB will help further that process, especially in a state in the Deep South, like Louisiana.

Local schools, whether traditional public schools or charter schools, as the education providers, need autonomy to make the changes that are necessary to increase student achievement. Consequently, there is a real problem, as evidenced by the volume of on-going desegregation litigation cases, that education providers need express authority to intervene at schools operated by non-unitary school districts. It has been proven repeatedly that one size does not fit all in educating children. As such, local schools must be empowered with the autonomy to make the changes that will most benefit their students.

The second aim of the tripartite partnership is to encourage community engagement in education. Multiple "white papers" from any number of local chambers of commerce provide empirical data to support the proposition that it takes more than a village to raise a child. It takes business involvement, too. In order to encourage local business involvement with local schools— especially charter schools—state legislatures should offer tax incentives. If the charter and education reform movement is to grow, it needs fertile soil. Legislative tax incentives would provide a natural link between local schools and local businesses and ensure that they each receive the support they need.

Finally, although not emphasized here, increased parental involvement is absolutely essential to closing the achievement gap. Legislative action is therefore necessary. Legislation that would create tax incentives for employers to allow employed parents/guardians/primary caretakers compensated time away from the workplace to participate in school-related activities would encourage familial involvement and presumably drive academic improvement. Incentive measures that facilitate familial involvement are necessary to achieve the collaborative atmosphere that is conducive to sustained education reform. To be successful in an on-going Movement with Black and other underprivileged children at its center, education reform must be holistic, not isolated.

The Social Necessity of NCLB

To understand the significance of what NCLB sought to reform, it is necessary to establish the condition of public education before NCLB's enactment. There are at least two sad truths about the pre-NCLB status of public education in the United States. First, the vertical gap between Black and White students significantly dropped over the last thirty-plus years. Second, the horizontal gap between Black and White students significantly increased, while overall standards and achievement uniformly plummeted.[274] This means that, notwithstanding previous governmental efforts to close the academic achievement gap between Black and White students, the average Black student continues to be left behind at alarming rates, when compared to the average White student.

With respect to the vertical drop, in recent years researchers have observed a uniform decrease in educational achievement among *all* students. A noted education researcher opines that:

> The data on student achievement in America during the past twenty-five years point to an inescapable conclusion: American student achievement today is barely at the level it was in the mid-1970s, and in many respects, student achievement is significantly lower than it was twenty-five years ago. Although we have tried our best to find alternative explanations for the decline, the evidence clearly shows that the achievement drop is genuine, substantial and pervasive across ethnic, socioeconomic, and age groups. Moreover, there is no indication from recent assessments that this situation is changing, and some indication, as evidenced in recent reports on declining SAT scores, that it is worsening once again. To top it all off, our definition of educational excellence has eroded nearly to the point of meaninglessness, and yet, only a handful of students qualify for the dubious distinction of placing in the top category. As my colleague Dan Koretz, writing for the Congressional Budget Office in 1986 concluded, the

existence of an "overall drop in the achievement [entailing] sizeable declines in higher-level skills, such as inference and problem-solving, is beyond question."[275]

There is an old saying that "[a] rising tide lifts all boats." Since the 1970s, the tide has been falling and all boats have been sinking. Sadly, this problem is particularly pronounced in the African American community.[276]

In discussing his research on educational achievement among various ethnic groups, Dr. Laurence Steinberg and his team of researchers noted:

> Although we did not intend our study to focus primarily on ethnic differences in achievement and other aspects of adolescent development, we were struck repeatedly by how significant a role ethnicity played in structuring young people's lives, both inside and outside of school. Youngsters' patterns of activities, interests and friendships were all influenced by their ethnic background. Moreover, we could not ignore the fact that students of different ethnic groups experienced markedly different degrees of success and failure in school.[277]

In specifically addressing the achievement gap between the subjects of his research, Dr. Steinberg wrote:

> [O]ne of the most consistent observations reported by social scientists who study achievement

in this country is that Asian-
American students perform, on
average, substantially better
than their [W]hite peers, who in
turn outperform their Black and
Latino counterparts. This finding
has emerged over and over again,
whether the index in question is
based on school grades or
performance on standardized
tests of achievement.[278]

Among Black school children, therefore, school
performance was apparently the worst, in comparison to
other ethnic groups. Indeed, the achievement gap is and
has been a very real and empirically measurable
phenomenon.

In light of this disappointing and empirically
discernable trend, the federal government has been
proactive in attempting to address the decline. For
example, according to authors Elaine Witty and Rod Paige
(former U.S. secretary of Education), the modern day
educational accountability reform movement began with
President George H.W. Bush's 1991 Education Summit,
with its policy recommendations later codified in President
William J. Clinton's Improving America's Schools Act of
1994.[279] Secretary Paige, the U.S. Secretary of Education
under whom NCLB became law, provided the following
assessment of NCLB's effect on the achievement gap:

The NCLB literally changed
the culture of public education
in the United States, and in
concert with other factors,
caused improvement primarily
in math and to a lesser extent
reading, especially for
minority populations.[280]

The classic political question in education reform almost always deals with money. It traditionally comes down to whether less is more or whether more is less. Consequently, while there are a variety of political and financial perspectives on the impact of government fiscal allocations on education reform, there are generally two broad camps: the "Increasers" and the "Changers."

Education reformers in the "Increaser" camp typically point to deficiencies in funding for school innovation, firmly believing that their programs would work if only they were adequately funded. Conversely, education reformers in the "Changer" camp typically argue that more money will not facilitate education reform. The following argument exemplifies the "Changer" perspective:

> Resource-based reforms have attempted to improve schools. They include such measures as increased funding, new textbooks, wiring schools for internet access, renovating or updating school facilities, reducing class sizes (more teachers per pupil), and other measures that require greater financial expenditures. Scholars have studied the relationship between per-student spending and achievement tests scores since the publication of the Equality of Educational Opportunity (better known at the Coleman Report) in 1966. Coleman, a leading sociologist, concluded that factors such as per pupil spending and class size do not have a significant impact on student achievement scores.

Yet, despite this and subsequent findings, many lawmakers and educators continue to believe that additional resources and funding will somehow eventually solve the problems within the educational system.

Economist Erik Hanushek and others have replicated Coleman's study and even extended it to international studies of student achievement. The finding of thirty-one years of research is clear: better education cannot be bought.[281]

There is much that can be said about the theoretical differences between the two camps. Rather than focusing on differences, however, Black children are demanding that education stakeholders find common ground and make the improvements they deserve. Attempted improvements have historically been through government.

ESEA, part of President Lyndon B. Johnson's Great Society initiative known as the "War on Poverty," was the Movement's major legislative accomplishment addressing inequity in public education. ESEA's initial goal was to provide enhanced funding to help solve the problems facing economically disadvantaged children.[282] Indeed, over the next thirty years, ESEA poured hundreds of billions of dollars into public education.[283]

ESEA delivers federal dollars to State Educational Agencies ("SEAs"),[284] which funnel money to local school boards (also known as Local Educational Agencies or "LEAs") to supplement educational objectives. While ESEA provides a variety of resources for LEAs, they receive the bulk of support through Title I funds, which help offset the extra cost of educating disadvantaged students.[285] With as many as 90% of public schools receiving Title I funds, its reach has been tremendous. [286]

Title I targets schools with high concentrations of low-income families, where federal funding is contingent upon eligible students failing to meet educational benchmarks. For the first fifteen years of its existence, Title I's goal was to ensure that economically disadvantaged children could perform at the basic level of achievement.[287] Unfortunately, the program failed to meet its goal.

Though ESEA was renewed with revisions on three occasions, education officials began to question the benefit of the program. As early as 1988, federal officials began to challenge its efficacy.[288] In 1994, under the leadership of President Bill Clinton, Congress passed the Improving America's Schools Act ("IASA"),[289] with the fundamental premise that all children could master challenging content and complex problem-solving skills when expectations are high, and that all children be given the opportunity to learn challenging material. Before IASA, LEAs could receive Title I funds under ESEA as long as they had enough eligible (*i.e.* poor) children in a system. After IASA, LEAs had to develop plans to increase achievement in order to receive funding.[290]

Even though success was measured at least annually through assessments and "any additional measures or indicators" that SEAs developed to track progress, students did not meet anticipated benchmarks. After the federal government poured in hundreds of billions of dollars over more than twenty-five years, American students still lagged behind their foreign peers. Indeed, education officials were unsuccessful in narrowing the achievement gap between Black and White students. The need was therefore obvious: Congress had to again act to address the achievement gap between Black and White children.

In the face of the growing achievement gap, President George W. Bush signed NCLB into law. NCLB's "supply-side reform...aims to create a more effective supply of educational services through the pressures of accountability and institutional reform."[291] The NCLB blueprint for reform incorporated four features: (1) stronger accountability for results; (2) greater flexibility for states, school districts and schools in the use of federal funds; (3) more choices for parents of children from disadvantaged backgrounds; and (4) an emphasis on teaching methods that have been demonstrated to work. It is helpful to review each feature here.

The Aims of the NCLB

NCLB mandates annual assessments in reading and math for students from third grade through eighth grade. Under NCLB, SEAs are responsible for developing the test for students, and states may not receive federal funds under Title I unless they have implemented acceptable plans to measure growth.[292] States are also required to publicize and disseminate the results of testing before the beginning of the next school year.[293] These annual "report cards" allow parents to compare schools and make informed decisions about educational options.

NCLB also provides more flexibility for LEAs in the use of Title I funds. Before NCLB, Title I money was targeted specifically for disadvantaged students. LEAs were not allowed to reduce funding for disadvantaged children and then offset that reduction with Title I funds.[294] Under NCLB, LEAs have the authority to transfer up to fifty percent of federal funding to other approved programs without separate approval. This flexibility, in theory, allows local schools to address their particular needs to enhance educational opportunities.

The schools "report cards" are designed to help parents make informed decisions about their children's education. Parental choice allows parents to act on those informed decisions. Parents of children in under-performing schools are given a broader range of options. If

119

a child's school fails to meet standards for two years, the child's parent(s) may choose to enroll the child in a higher performing school (including a charter school). Local school districts are required to provide transportation. Students attending schools that fail to meet standards for three years may receive supplemental services like summer school, after school services, and/or tutoring.

All teachers hired after NCLB and working in programs supported by Title I funds must be "highly qualified."[295] NCLB funds may also be used to support scientifically based instruction in reading programs.[296] Indeed, NCLB aims to improve the quality of education by also providing opportunities for the professional development of teachers.[297] Moreover, it promotes "school wide reform" by ensuring access "to effective, scientifically based instructional strategies and challenging academic content."[298]

NCLB aims to provide more choice for parents and students by relying on market forces to shape school improvement. The practical effect of NCLB on a national scale was much more complicated, due to differences in state systems and varying degrees of local school board control. NCLB's effects in Louisiana, however, are a good example to consider and highlight here.

Education Reform in Louisiana

In conducting an informal broad-based national survey to determine which state has adopted the most reform-oriented initiatives to change the education paradigm, Minnesota, Michigan, Arizona, and Louisiana were considered because of the proliferation of charter schools in those states since NCLB's enactment. Ultimately, however, looking at the intricacies of Louisiana's public school system in the context of the 50th anniversary of the Movement's legislative achievements in 1964 is arguably most appropriate for several reasons, including the fact that Louisiana is a southern state with many segregated school districts, and its efforts to rebuild the Orleans Parish School System ("OPSS") in the aftermath of Hurricane Katrina ("Katrina") have received national attention.

Furthermore, NCLB arguably has a unique effect on Louisiana for at least two reasons. First, New Orleans and the OPSS are the subject of what has been deemed "the great experiment," because New Orleans is the first majority charter school city in the United States. Second, because Louisiana has so many segregated school districts operating under federal district court supervision in ongoing desegregation litigation, school choice, under NCLB, is really at the discretion of the federal judiciary.

As a foundational matter, the reader has already seen anecdotal as well as empirical data supporting the proposition that NCLB was motivated by a desire to remedy racial issues in education. Indeed, the United States has a sordid history on the subject of race, as does Louisiana, a state in the Deep South.

In looking at Louisiana specifically, it is interesting to explore the interplay between race, education reform and the Recovery School District established there. In response to NCLB's passage and enactment in 2001, the Louisiana Legislature passed Act 9 during its 2003 legislative session and created the Recovery School District ("RSD"). Pursuant to Act 9, the RSD is legally empowered to takeover and operate failed public schools after a state Board of Elementary and Secondary (BESE") vote and to control and expend the LSD's share of its state and local dollars. This reform measure in Louisiana, passed during the state's first general/non-fiscal legislative session after NCLB was enacted, has been a great source of controversy because of the inherent politics of race regarding who controls the resources to help Black school children.

According to Louisiana state law, once a local school is deemed academically unacceptable for a period of four consecutive years, "the school *shall be removed* from the jurisdiction of the local school board . . . and transferred to the jurisdiction of the Recovery School District . . ."[299] Act 9 also created the controversial Type 5 charter school model whereby the RSD contracts with a non-profit group which assumes day-to-day responsibility for managing the failed school[300] According to statute, Type 5 charter schools are preexisting public schools transferred to the RSD after a state takeover and are required to maintain open admission policies.

In addition to individual schools, the state legislature has authorized the RSD to assume control of entire school districts if they are deemed to be academically unacceptable or "districts in crisis."[301] In the wake of Katrina, the OPSS was deemed a "district in crisis," and 107 of the 116 public schools in New Orleans were subject to state takeover. In chronicling this sequence, University of South Carolina law professor Danielle Holley-Walker wrote:

> On August 29, 2005, Hurricane Katrina began its devastation of the city of New Orleans and eventually became the worst natural disaster in United States history. In the wake of the storm, the New Orleans schools were in disarray-students and teachers dislocated, buildings damaged, and the school district administration disorganized and scattered throughout the United States. Ultimately, the Orleans Parish school board issued public statements that it would not be able to reopen the New Orleans public schools that school year.

Due to these circumstances, Governor Kathleen Blanco determined that in order to reopen New Orleans' public schools in the 2005-2006 school year, the state would have to fill the gap left by the local school board. In order to provide the state with the necessary authority to oversee the local schools, a November 2005 special session of the Louisiana legislature expanded the definition of a 'failed' school under the Recovery School District Act. Previously a 'failed' school under the RSDA was a school that was deemed 'academically unacceptable' for four consecutive years. Once a school had "failed," it would be placed under the auspices of the RSD, to be administered and controlled by the state instead of the local school board. In the November 2005 special session, the legislature expanded the definition of "failed" school to include all schools that scored below the state average and that were operated in school systems designated as being in "Academic Crisis." Based on this new definition, 107 schools previously organized in the Orleans Parish School District were transferred to the control of the RSD.[302]

This drastic reform measure in New Orleans has also been the subject of great controversy because of its perceived racial overtones, given the timing of it. New Orleans was a White-controlled city until the 1980s when its first Black mayor, Ernest N. "Dutch" Morial, was elected. There were three succeeding Black mayors of New Orleans, including Morial's son, who heads the National Urban League. Each mayor, Sydney Bartholomew, Marc Morial, and Ray Nagin, served eight-years in office. In the city's first municipal election after Katrina, when many Blacks were forced to leave the city and unable to return, Mitch Landrieu, a white lawyer and politician, and son of the last White mayor to govern New Orleans before Dutch Morial was elected, was elevated to the city's highest office. The transfer of the Orleans Parish schools to the RSD occurred as the racial dynamic of the transfer of mayoral power from Black to White was taking place. This led some to perceive a race-based motive at play in the two concomitant events.

Because the increasing prevalence of charter schools seen across the country is particularly pronounced in Louisiana, understandably, the reform-oriented question raised by Louisianans was whether charter schools are right and will be effective for educating Black children. In January of 2009, BESE accepted the recommendation of Louisiana's then superintendent of Education and voted to take over many schools, transferring them to the RSD. In the capital city of Baton Rouge alone, BESE voted to assume operational control of eight out of twelve eligible schools. Shortly thereafter, the superintendent announced his plans to issue Type 5 charters to non-profit entities for the day-to-day management and operation of the "failed" schools. Without question, the state bringing in out-of-state organizations to manage local schools caused widespread tension, especially along racial and socioeconomic lines. With many White-run, out-of-state groups being presented as having the answer to problems dealing primarily with Black children, the post-Katrina racial tension increased.

Prior to Katrina, the OPSS was the worst performing school district in Louisiana. It was in noted financial disarray and was the subject of a federal investigation of alleged fraud and corruption. After the takeover by the RSD and the influx of charter schools, New Orleans now has the largest percentage of charter schools and the largest percentage of public school students attending charter schools of any school district in the United States. It is apparently clear that public school transformation in Louisiana—indeed, across the United States—will be facilitated by the charter school movement only if charter schools develop into great schools for at risk children. The educational legacy of the Movement deserves nothing less.

Desegregation Efforts in Louisiana

Despite recent academic improvement in Louisiana, the state's public educational system is still plagued by the consequences of the Jim Crow laws that served as a catalyst for the Movement. Moreover, the state's on-going efforts to improve public education are undermined by a backdrop of natural catastrophes, including Katrina and the *BP Deepwater Horizon* explosion and oil spill, poverty, and on-going desegregation cases where school districts have failed to meet unitary standards. These are clearly examples of long-term problems that require sustained long-term solutions.

In describing Louisiana's economic challenges, politicians often refer to the state as "land rich and cash poor." The percentage of children living in poverty in Louisiana is higher per capita than the per capita percentage of children living in poverty nationally. More than two-thirds of Louisiana's public school students live in low-income households, compared with twenty-three percent of public school children nationally. This phenomenon is most remarkable when considered in conjunction with the fact that Louisiana's K-12 enrollment has significantly dropped over the last several years and is predicted to continually do so, while the state's non-public school enrollment has traditionally been double the national average of 10%. Not surprisingly, there is a higher concentration of Black students in Louisiana's public schools, exacerbating the problem of racial poverty. While more affluent Whites are opting out of public education, poor Black children are overwhelmingly populating the classrooms. This phenomenon presents a significant challenge leading to an inherently segregated public school system.

Shockingly, over fifty years after *Brown v. Board,* numerous school districts in Louisiana remain mired in on-going school desegregation lawsuits that were originally filed in the 1950s and 1960s. According to a September 2007 report from the United States Commission on Civil Rights, forty-two school districts in Louisiana have on-going desegregation cases pending in federal courts.[303] Desegregation cases present a significant obstacle to education reform groups as they seek to improve public education and expand charter schools, because desegregation cases *are not* about academic improvement. Instead and in accordance with *Brown v. Board,* such cases are about achieving racial parity in school systems.[304]

After the Supreme Court's ruling in *Brown,* that *de jure* segregation in public schools was an unconstitutional violation of the Equal Protection Clause of Amendment XIV of the United States Constitution, many states—especially those in the South—along with local school districts, ignored or actively resisted the Court's ruling. A decade after the landmark decision, few school districts had taken any steps to implement any racial desegregation programs. Consequently, many litigants filed suit against their local school boards and/or school systems requesting that the federal courts enjoin both *de jure* and/or *de facto* school segregation. In Louisiana, where forty-two of the local school districts had not been declared unitary by the respective federal district courts, many litigants filed similar lawsuits seeking injunctions.

By the late 1960s, little had changed as a result of the Supreme Court's order to desegregate public schools "with all deliberate speed." After *Brown*, many cases addressing alleged ambiguities in the *Brown* Court's dictate to desegregate public schools worked their way up to the Supreme Court. Most notably in its opinion *Green v. County School Board of New Kent County*, issued in 1968 only a month after Martin Luther King, Jr.'s assassination, the Supreme Court emphasized the respective district courts responsibility to compel school districts to operate integrated schools.

Green held that federal courts should monitor school systems until the vestiges of *de jure* segregation were eliminated and spurred widespread federal court supervision of school districts and/or school boards that were operating "dual" school systems. Thus, under *Green*, federal courts are required, to the extent practical, to evaluate every facet of school operation to ensure local school systems are making good faith efforts to transition from a dual system to one that is unitary in order to be released from federal court supervision.

Green established specific standards by which desegregation efforts could be judged. Consequently, assessing whether a school district had eliminated the vestiges of *de jure* segregation, federal courts must, to the extent practical, look at every facet of school operations. In particular, the *Green* Court identified six (6) factors that should be examined:

(1) student assignment;
(2) faculty assignment;
(3) staff assignment;
(4) transportation;
(5) extracurricular activities; and
(6) facilities.

Additionally, for the first time, the Supreme Court used the term "unitary" to describe a school system that had transitioned from a segregated, racially dual system, to a unitary, desegregated system.

In the 1970s, after having ordered that desegregation should proceed without further delay, the Supreme Court's rulings focused on how to implement *Green*.[305] Arguably, busing was and remains the most hotly contested measure of implementation promulgated by the Supreme Court in the decades after *Green*.

Because the *Green* Court did not provide clear guidelines as to when federal court supervision should end, in the early 1990s, the Supreme Court revisited its general standards for unitary status in *Board of Education of Oklahoma City Public Schools v. Dowell* and *Freeman v. Pitts*. In *Dowell*, the Court ruled that a declaration of unitary status is appropriate if a school district demonstrates that it has complied with a judicial desegregation order since it was entered and the vestiges of past discrimination are eliminated. In *Freeman*, however, the Court expanded the scope of *Dowell* by holding that school districts do not need to achieve unitary status as to all aspects of school administration to obtain partial relief in those areas in which success has been achieved. Together, *Dowell* and *Freeman* provide the most current roadmap for school districts seeking unitary status to re-obtain control of their school systems, with *Green* providing the basis for both decisions.

In *Freeman v. Pitts*, the Supreme Court ruled that courts might incrementally remove judicial supervision in favor of local control. The Court also opined that the *Green* factors should not be a rigid framework and noted that courts may conduct an inquiry into the quality of education to determine whether other elements of the school system are in need of judicial supervision to ensure full compliance with the consent decree. In other words, while very significant, the *Green* factors are not the only consideration in determining whether unitary and/or partial unitary status should be declared. As such, the practical effect of a pending desegregation order is that federal regulations like

NCLB are not necessarily applicable. Judges *may* allow local school districts to participate in reform efforts, but judicial oversight is a complicating circumstance that could ultimately rob local school districts or reform-oriented states, like Louisiana, of the opportunity to implement NCLB's reform model.

Moving Education Reform Forward

The question is now "Where do we go from here?" As shown, educational reform under NCLB has been fraught with challenges in Louisiana, an example of a state that is attempting to help young Black children, while still caught in the aftermath of history of racial division. As the on-going Movement continues, how do contemporary activists accept the keys of legacy and responsibility and work to provide Black children with the opportunity for success they so absolutely deserve? It is now time to address the shortcomings of the previous reforms.

As an initial matter, Congress should require state legislatures and local school districts to modify teacher tenure laws as a condition for Title I funding. The path to success and achieving equality in public education *does not* involve cutting back on NCLB's provisions. Instead, Congress should take more steps forward to enhance the effectiveness of the current reform agenda.

It is undisputed that teachers perform a vital service to society, and that the value of their experience should not be underestimated. However, like any other professional, teachers must go when they are ineffective, and that determination must be made on an empirical rather than political basis under NCLB. Federal law already protects older teachers from ageism. The burden should rest on the employee to show that his or her removal was unlawful, not on the school system to prove that the discharge was lawful.

Second, Congress should mandate a plan and method of regularly assessing the performance of school board members and superintendents in developing better school environments. Teachers should not be the only parties subject to review under NCLB. Local school board members, superintendents and central office administrators should be subject to the same "scientifically proven" methods for measuring success. Districts with failing schools, high dropout rates and low returns for taxpayer investments must also be subject to review. If the single greatest predictor of a child's academic success is school environment, NCLB must assess the performance of board members, superintendents and central office administrators in developing better school environments.

Third, as a condition of receiving Title I funding, Congress should require that states provide local school boards with the tools to assess superintendent performance. States must identify the number of board members and the essential skills they must possess to maximize district performance. States must help local districts minimize administrative red tape and maximize administrator performance.

In our effort to accept the keys of legacy and responsibility to move the education reform component of the Movement along, we *must* support legislation that embraces and commits to implementing the foregoing three areas of emphasis. We can do so by lobbying and voting for politicians that make these commitments. We can also volunteer with local groups to mentor young people in character development, as well as pooling together human and capital resources to support their educational development. In accepting the keys, we all are called to action.

Chapter 10

The Impatient Act of Waiting

(A Sermon Originally Shared with Greater Mount Carmel Baptist Church in Baton Rouge, Louisiana)

For you yourselves know very well that the day of the Lord will come like a thief in the night. When they say, "There is peace and security," then sudden destruction will come upon them, as labor pains come upon a pregnant woman, and there will be no escape! But you, beloved, are not in darkness, for that day to surprise you like a thief; for you are all children of light and children of the day; we are not of the night or of darkness. So then, let us not fall asleep as others do, but let us keep awake and be sober; for those who sleep, sleep at night and those who are drunk get drunk at night. But since we belong to the day, let us keep sober and put on the breastplate of faith and love, and for a helmet, the hope of salvation. For God has destined us not for wrath, but for obtaining salvation through our Lord Jesus Christ, who died for us, so that whether we are awake or asleep we may live with him.

And we urge you, beloved, to admonish the idlers, encourage the fainthearted, help the weak, be patient with all of them. See that none of you repays evil for evil, but always seek to do good to one another and to all. Rejoice always, pray without ceasing, give thanks in all circumstances, for this is the will of God in Christ Jesus for you.

- *First Thessalonians* 5: 2-10 & 14-15 (NRSV)

Before the death of Rev. Dr. Martin Luther King, Jr., in 1968, a book was compiled with some of Dr. King's most significant writings and speeches. It was called *Why We Can't Wait*. As you would imagine, the book included a transcript of Dr. King's famous "I have a Dream" speech. Most significant to me, however, is the fact that it included a copy of his famous 1963 letter, essentially a mini-treatise on civil disobedience, called "Letter From Birmingham Jail."

The *Letter From Birmingham Jail* was written while he was in jail in Birmingham, Alabama for using the First Amendment to protest against the discriminatory things he deemed unjust. In responding to criticism from fellow members of the clergy, King noted that the South's "slow down clergy" called his actions "unwise and untimely." In responding to those members of the clergy that wanted to simply wait for an end to Jim Crow segregation and allow the status quo to be maintained, King noted the urgency of "now" by indicating there simply was no more time to wait. King had grown impatient with waiting.

Although, I admit, that I have never been to jail in Birmingham, I know a little something about impatient waiting, too. Last year, for example, as I was preparing for a return flight to get back to the South, I was in a rush. I arrived at the airport early to ensure there would be no issues. Unfortunately for me, however, I found out the flight was delayed. I went to the counter, looking at my watch, and asked a very kind flight attendant how quickly we would be boarding. The attendant responded very politely and said, "Sir, I'm sorry for the delay. If you'll just be patient we should be boarding soon." A few minutes later, when there was still no boarding, I returned to the counter and asked again, how long was the delay and if there was an update. The flight attendant politely apologized for my inconvenience and promised that if I could just be a little more "patient" my wait wouldn't be too much longer.

After several minutes, as I was tempted to return to the counter and inquire again as to the flight's status, I learned first-hand that the worst thing about being told to be "patient" is realizing there's absolutely nothing you can do when you're required to wait. Patient waiting, as I learned, occurs when one is required to sit by in a state of inaction, unable to assist with the flow of events. By definition, therefore, patient waiting requires one to be a non-active observer. What I'm trying to say is that patient waiting requires inaction. It requires that that non-engaged participant sit by and simply wait without any meaningful opportunity to act. For King, the other members of the clergy that motivated him writing *Letter From Birmingham Jail* wanted him to patiently sit there and just wait for Congress to pass a Civil Rights Act. They wanted him to patiently sit there and wait for Congress to pass a Voting Rights Act. In my case, the polite flight attendant wanted me to patiently sit there and wait to board the plane. Those are real life examples of so-called "patient waiting."

Now that we have a basis of comparison for the patient act of waiting, I want to talk for just a little bit about what I like to call the "impatient act of waiting." In doing so, by way of outline, I want to talk with you about three specific things. First, I want to talk a little about the Apostle Paul's understanding of the "impatient act of waiting." Second, in the context of our celebration of Black History Month, I want to talk a little about how the Christian church's recent history of action is the very essence of "the impatient act of waiting." And third, in building upon our celebrated history, I want to talk a little about how Jesus' church of today—50-years after King exhibited the impatient act of waiting in Birmingham— must continue the legacy of impatience that Jesus passed on to Peter and that King passes on to us. As we attempt to build on the legacy of Jesus' church and serve God's children today, the church must engage in "the impatient act of waiting."

By way of background, it's important to know a little about Paul, the author of *First Thessalonians*. Paul was a Pharisaic Jew who had a life-changing experience while traveling on a road to Damascus.[306] He was headed to persecute Jesus' followers when Jesus himself called Paul to preach the gospel to the Gentiles. In other words, Paul was called to travel throughout the Mediterranean and around the Greco-Roman world to found new churches in different colonies, by bearing witness to non-Jewish communities. One of the churches he founded was the church at Thessalonica.

First Thessalonians was written shortly after Paul's first visit to Thessalonica, after establishing a new church at Philippi, approximately one hundred miles away. While traveling, Paul received word from Timothy, his understudy and son in the ministry, regarding the young church at Thessalonica. Because Thessalonica was a port city, along the Aegean Sea—much like New Orleans is a port city along the Mississippi River—Thessalonica had lots of visitors and lots of cultural influences. In addressing some of the young church's concerns and questions, Paul wrote to it a letter, the Greek work for which is "epistle," as what biblical scholars regard as not only the first of all of Paul's epistles, but also the oldest document that was later complied into what we now know as the New Testament of the Holy Bible.

Paul's focus in *First Thessalonians*, the first biblical document written after Jesus' death and resurrection, was what he called in the Greek: the *parousia* or the Second Coming of Christ. Accordingly, in looking at Paul's epistles—especially looking at *First Thessalonians*—because the focus is on waiting for the Second Coming, Paul admonishes believers to be engaged in an "impatient act of waiting" because he believed the Second Coming was imminent or that it literally was going to happen any day.

As an example of Paul's "urgency of now" theology, in *First Corinthians*, Chapter 7, Paul actually discourages marriage and child bearing because he simply doesn't think there's time. For Paul, because Jesus' return is imminent—not just now, but *right now*—believers simply can't afford to sit by and engage in the patient act of waiting. No. No. No. For Paul, waiting was the ultimate act of impatience. Paul wants us to prepare for Christ's Second Coming by being more like Christ, the outward manifestation of what it means to be a Christian.

In writing *First Thessalonians*, if Paul is trying to encourage the young church to be more like Christ in impatiently waiting for Christ's anticipated return, it begs the question what sort of ministry did Christ lead when he was here on earth. In my humble estimation, Jesus Christ was the first social justice preacher. The gospel narratives tell us that when Jesus came from the wilderness and began his public ministry, he went to the Jewish synagogue and read from the scroll of the prophet Isaiah proclaiming that he came to give sight to the blind; to set the captives free; and to release the oppressed.[307] In other words, during the years of Jesus' Earthly ministry, he too was engaged in the impatient act of waiting because he demonstrated a call to action while waiting to fulfill the very purpose for his existence: to die for the sins of humanity and reconcile humans to right relation with God.

When we look at the text, considering Paul's understanding that Jesus was indeed coming back and coming back very soon, Paul is telling the young church members in Thessalonica to get their lives together and get their houses in order. If you look then at the text's figurative meaning or *symbolic meaning* in Chapter 5, Paul is telling Christian believers that they don't live in the darkness of confusion; instead, they live in the daylight of understanding. Jesus will come again. In Chapter 5, verse 6, Paul admonishes those that live in the light of God to not fall asleep as others do. Instead, keep awake and keep sober. In other words, while living in the light of Christ, don't go to the inaction of a patient act of waiting. Don't go to the intoxicated state of complacency. Instead, pray without ceasing. Be alert. Be ready and be engaged in what I like to call the impatient act of waiting!

With Paul's understanding of the impatient act of waiting as a foundation, we can move on to see how we as spiritual descendents of the young church at Thessalonica have carried on the earthly ministry of Jesus Christ by discussing the church's active role in the impatient act of waiting. In the spirit of the social activism that defined the Earthly ministry of Jesus Christ, the modern day church must too give sight to the blind; release the captives; and set the oppressed free. In other words, my brothers and sisters, the "social gospel" reminds us that the church must not only be concerned with the glory of the kingdom to come, but must also be concerned with the inequities of the kingdom at hand. The church's actions in working in the kingdom at hand must, therefore, define the impatient act of waiting. That's the legacy of action Jesus gave to Peter and the same legacy King and the Movement passes on to us.

When we think about the impatient act of waiting and the church's recent role in addressing the kingdom at hand, we have so much for which we should be proud that results from impatient waiting down here in South Louisiana.

Before a young preacher named Martin Luther King, Jr. was catapulted to national attention because of his impatient act of waiting in Montgomery, Alabama in 1955, Jesus' church came together to deal with the injustices of the kingdom at hand by leading a social gospel in the Baton Rouge Bus Boycott. That boycott was a continuation of the ministry of the same Jesus who came to set the oppressed free. In being practitioners of a social gospel, therefore, the church has a legacy and proud history of engaging in the impatient act of waiting, dealing not only with the salvation in the kingdom to come, but also injustices in the kingdom at hand.

The impatient act of waiting resulted in successes in the Baton Rouge Bus Boycott of 1953, the Montgomery Bus Boycott of 1955 and the Tallahassee Bus Boycott of 1956. The Black church led all those movements. But watch this: the church's impatient act of waiting wasn't just limited to economic boycotts in protest against social injustices. In the spirit of Jesus Christ, the one who suffered for all, the church's history of practicing the impatient act of waiting also manifested with a willingness to suffer on behalf of others, too.

Members of the church showed the impatient act of waiting when they staged lunch counter sit-ins in 1961 in Greensboro, North Carolina; organized the Freedom Rides on Greyhound and Trailways Buses, from Washington, DC down to New Orleans; and, in the most popularly recognized act of selfless suffering, got together on Sunday, March 7, 1965 at Morris Brown Chapel African Methodist Episcopal Church in Selma, Alabama—after having received First Sunday communion—and assembled for a march across the Edmund Pettis Bridge to show impatience and demand a voting rights bill to fight against the injustices of the kingdom at hand. That's the impatient act of waiting. After being beaten by police officers, attached by dogs, and sprayed with fire hoses, the impatient act of waiting resulted in the election of Blacks to the United States Congress. The impatient act if waiting led to the election of Blacks as mayors and members of city councils. The impatient act of waiting even led to the election of America's first Black president, the Honorable Barack Obama. Yes; the church has a proud history of building upon the earthly ministry of Jesus Christ and following through on Paul's challenge to the Thessalonians. Indeed, the church has a proud history of being engaged in the impatient act of waiting.

Today, my brothers and sisters, as we continue to celebrate Black History Month, we have an opportunity to rededicate ourselves to carrying out the ministry of Jesus Christ. As we build upon the Apostle Paul's charge to the Thessalonians to engage in the impatient act of waiting, and the church's successful history of being engaged in the impatient act of waiting, the question I pose to each and every one of you is will you, too, engage in the impatient act of waiting?

In other words, will you rededicate yourselves to the mission of not only this church, but to the continuing ministry of Jesus Christ? Will you rededicate yourselves to giving sight to the blind? Will you rededicate yourselves to releasing the captives? Will you rededicate to setting the oppressed free? That's the only way today's church can respond to today's challenges and engage in the impatient act of waiting.

In other words, what I'm trying to ask is whether you rededicate Jesus' church to a feeding ministry or a job skills training ministry for ex-offenders. That's the impatient act of waiting. Will you rededicate yourself to Paul's call to those that live in the light of day, by praying without ceasing and doing good for one another? Will you rededicate yourself to a social gospel that deals not only with salvation in the kingdom to come but also the needs of the kingdom at hand? The question I pose to you today, my brothers and sisters, is to what will you rededicate yourselves? Will you rededicate yourselves to the mission of Jesus' church as we react to situations in our current-day community, just as Paul reacted to situations in his ancient-day Thessalonica? Will you commit to the impatient act of waiting?

We can't go back and re-cross the Edmund Pettis Bridge. We now have the right to vote. But since we have the right to vote, will you as a Christian church commit to voter registration drives in an effort to give sight to the blind, release the captives, and set the oppressed free?

In federal elections in the House and Senate, will you commit to not only voting but to bringing someone else to vote, too? Will you commit to not only driving to the polls but also driving someone else, too? That's the only way, my brothers and sisters, we can "give sight to the blind, release the captives, and make sure the oppressed go free."

In this day and age where school reform has become almost a household buzzword, will you commit as a church to become actively involved with public education? I'm not talking about "patient waiting." I'm talking about the *impatient act of waiting*. I'm asking if you are willing to sit by in a state of inaction and watch schools fail while not getting involved? Will you sit by and watch schools continue to be taken over without having a say? No. No. No. That's not was Jesus called you to do. That's not what Paul wrote about doing. That's not what the Christian church has historically done and it's not what the church can afford to do today. We have a proud history of engaging in the impatient act of waiting.

Don't get caught on the sidelines where you can do nothing. Don't be stuck in an airport waiting to board your plane. Somebody here is saying, "Put me in the game coach. I can't sit by and just watch anymore. Get me off the bench." Will you be engaged in the impatient act of waiting? That's the legacy you're required to uphold. Are you up to the task? Don't be with the "slow down" clergy that discouraged King. Be prepared to accept your role in serving society now. Show how that social gospel is alive and well. That's what I call the impatient act of waiting.

139

NOTE: The citations below generally conform with typical legal citation standards, as exemplified in *The Bluebook: A Uniform System of Citation.*

1.   VINCENT HARDING, HOPE AND HISTORY: WHY WE MUST SHARE THE STORY OF THE MOVEMENT 98 (1990) (emphasis added) (discussing the theology of hope that permeated the civil disobedience during the Civil Rights Movement).
2.   *See* DAVID J. GARROW, BEARING THE CROSS: MARTIN LUTHER KING, JR. AND THE SOUTHERN CHRISTIAN LEADERSHIP CONFERENCE 127–28 (1986) [hereinafter "GARROW, BEARING THE CROSS"] at 97 (discussing King's proposal to name the civil rights organization the Southern *Christian* Leadership Conference "to emphasize that most of its participants and its potential popular base came from the black church").
3.   It bears noting that the Montgomery boycott was not the first of its kind. Two years earlier, in Baton Rouge, Louisiana, Blacks also boycotted city busses as a means of economic pressure. Based on willingness to compromise on the parts of both Black and White citizens, Rev. T.J. Jemison and Baton Rouge's Black ministerial leadership succeeded in establishing a "first come, first served" segregated seating. Under this arrangement, White passengers took seats from the front of the bus going toward the rear, while Blacks seated themselves from the rear toward the front. It eliminated the more objectionable features of bus segregation: Blacks having to surrender their places to Whites or being compelled to stand while reserved "white" seats remained empty. *See* ADAM FAIRCLOUGH, TO REDEEM THE SOUL OF AMERICA: THE SOUTHERN LEADERSHIP CONFERENCE AND MARTIN LUTHER KING, JR. (1987) at pg. 11–12. *See also* ANTOINE L. JOSEPH, THE DYNAMICS OF RACIAL PROGRESS: ECONOMIC INEQUALITY AND RACE RELATIONS SINCE RECONSTRUCTION 120 (2005)(discussing the popularity of the Baton Rouge, Louisiana bus boycott of 1953 and how it was overshadowed by the publicity generated from the arguments leading up to the Supreme Court's historic May 17, 1954, decision in *Brown v. Board of Education*, 347 U.S. 483 (1954)).
4.   After the Montgomery boycott's success, segregationists in Alabama successfully sought an injunction prohibiting the NAACP from operating within the state. When the NAACP opposed the injunction, the state of Alabama

successfully sought disclosure of the NAACP's membership lists. *See,* MARK V. TUSHNET, MAKING CIVIL RIGHTS LAW: THURGOOD MARSHALL AND THE SUPREME COURT, 1936–1961, 283–84 (1994). On appeal, however, the Supreme Court reversed. NAACP v. Alabama, 377 U.S. 288 (1964).

    5.   As Georgetown law professor Anthony Cook wrote: "Evangelical liberalism, from its theory of human nature, deduced a new role for the Church and for Christians. Given intrinsic human goodness, social institutions could and should be transformed to reflect more accurately the ideals of universal kinship and cooperation. An infallible scripture reflecting the static will of God could not justify social institutions like slavery and segregation." *See,* Anthony E. Cook, *Beyond Critical Legal Studies: The Reconstructive Theology of Dr. Martin Luther King, Jr., in* CRITICAL RACE THEORY: THE KEY WRITINGS THAT FORMED THE MOVEMENT at 95 (Kimberlé Crenshaw et al., eds. 1995) (originally published at 103 HARV. L. REV. 985 (1990)). Furthermore, as other scholarship notes, "'the formative religious traditions of the Western world—Judaism and Christianity—have for millennia embraced the conviction that their religious duty entailed active intervention in the 'body politic.' As a result . . . 'churches and synagogues can no more be silent on public issues than human beings can refrain from breathing.'" Daniel O. Conkle, *Secular Fundamentalism, Religious Fundamentalism, and the Search for Truth in Contemporary America, in* LAW & RELIGION: A CRITICAL ANTHOLOGY at 326 (Stephen M. Feldman, ed. 2000) (internal citations omitted). Moreover, King was influenced by the theology of Walter Rauschenbusch, a Baptist minister and professor of church history, who "believed that the American democracy undergirded by Christian morality represented a new era of social progress." Janet Forsythe Fishburn, *Walter Rauschenbusch and "The Woman Movement": A Gender Analysis, in* GENDER AND THE SOCIAL GOSPEL at 71 (Wendy J. Deichmann Edwards & Carolyn De Swarte Gifford, eds. 2003). Further, King also credited his studies of Rauschenbusch and Gandhi's ethics of nonviolence as a basis for his social views. *See* Michael Dwayne Blackwell, *In the Legacy of Martin Luther King, Jr.: the Social Gospel of Faye Wattleton and Marian Wright Edelman, in* GENDER AND THE SOCIAL GOSPEL 217 (Wendy J. Deichmann Edwards & Carolyn De Swarte Gifford, eds. 2003).

141

6.   Indeed, with respect to the church's role in society, Cook also writes that "unlike the dichotomy of conservative evangelicalism, there was a necessary relationship between the sacred and the secular, the Church and social issues." Cook, *supra* note 5, at 95.

7.   *Id.* (recognizing that it was necessary for "[t]he social gospel [to] turn…Christian attention [away] from the glories of the kingdom to come to the injustices of the kingdom at hand"). *See also* ALBERT J. RABOTEAU, CANAAN LAND: A RELIGIOUS HISTORY OF AFRICAN AMERICANS 124 (2001) ("The churches not only reacted to social and political change; they also participated in making it happen."). Further, at the end of the successful Montgomery boycott, King himself remarked about the church's "old order" passing away as the church moved toward stressing a social gospel as well as a gospel of salvation. *See also* CHARLES MARSH, GOD'S LONG SUMMER: STORIES OF FAITH AND CIVIL RIGHTS (1997) (discussing the role of faith and the church's developing social gospel, with a focus on the national events occurring in Mississippi during the summer of 1964).

8.   PETER J. PARIS, BLACK RELIGIOUS LEADERS: CONFLICT IN UNITY 120–21 (1991) (emphasis added).

9.   King, *Letter from Birmingham Jail* in Martin Luther King, Jr., WHY WE CAN'T WAIT, 82 (1968).

10.   *Id.* (emphasis added). One can also logically argue that as a Baptist minister, King's willingness to break laws for a noble cause was patterned after Jesus' violation of the Hebrew laws prohibiting work on the Sabbath, as done during his public ministry. *See, e.g., Matthew* 12:9–15. Accordingly, King's Judeo-Christian theology and associated willingness to accept the consequences of breaking unjust laws shows that "[t]he philosophy of civil disobedience embodies the recognition that obligations beyond those of the law might compel law breaking, but the doctrine steers that impulse toward a tightly-cabined form of illegal protest nevertheless consistent with respect to the rule of law." Matthew R. Hall, *Guilty But Civilly Disobedient: Reconciling Civil Disobedience and the Rule of Law*, 28 CARDOZO L. REV. 2083 (2007).

11.   FAIRCLOUGH, *supra* note 3, at 16.

12.   *See generally* 2 JUSTO L. GONZÁLEZ, THE STORY OF CHRISTIANITY: THE REFORMATION TO THE PRESENT DAY 485

(2010) (discussing King, the SCLC, and direct action during the Movement).

13. Ironically, notwithstanding such philosophy, many Christians justified racial discrimination, including the institution of slavery, under the so-called Curse of Ham detailed in *Genesis* 9. *See generally* DAVID M. WHITFORD, THE CURSE OF HAM IN THE EARLY MODERN ERA: THE BIBLE AND THE JUSTIFICATION FOR SLAVERY 1–2 (2009) (discussing former U.S. Senator Robert Byrd's opposition to the Civil Rights Act of 1964 and his justification of Jim Crow segregation based on *Genesis* 9:18–27); George H. Taylor, *Race, Religion, and the Law: The Tension Between Spirit and Its Institutionalization*, 6 U. MD. L.J. RACE, RELIGION, GENDER & CLASS 51, 52 (2006) ("Biblical predicates for racist claims by White Christians include the condemnation by Noah of his son Ham's progeny, due to Ham's misconduct. The book of *Genesis* quotes Noah saying of Ham's son, Canaan: 'Cursed be Canaan; a slave of slaves shall he be to his brothers.'") (quoting *Genesis* 9:25 (RSV)); *Numbers 25* (detailing the violence instituted because of interracial relations between the children Israel and other nations). Professor Anthony Cook credits King's theological studies as providing the foundation upon which he was able to deconstruct the logic of both "biblically-based racists," like *Genesis* 9 justifiers, and the "slow down clergy," like those who sent their written criticism to which King responded in writing *Letter From a Birmingham Jail*: The evangelicalism of George Washington Davis, King's professor of theology at Crozer Seminary, and the social gospel of Walter Rauschenbusch gave King the theological perspectives to challenge conservative evangelicalism's conception of human nature and its debilitating dichotomy between the spiritual and the secular, as well as between order and freedom. Evangelical liberalism turned conservative evangelicalism's conception of human nature on its head and called into question the universality of that theology's assumptions. Evangelical liberalism posited the goodness of human nature, as reflected in and resulting from human moral reasoning, and it conjectured that evil institutions had limited people's efforts to pursue the ideal of the Kingdom of Value, what King would later call the "Beloved Community." Cook, *supra* note 5, at 95.

14. PARIS, *supra* note 8, at 113.

15.   Walker v. City of Birmingham, 388 U.S. 307
(1967).
16.   *Walker*, 388 U.S. at 321–22; LESLIE C. GRIFFIN,
LAW AND RELIGION: CASES AND MATERIALS 170–71 (2d ed.
2010) (discussing King's stance on civil disobedience, the Supreme
Court's decision in *Walker v. City of Birmingham* and King's
Letter From Birmingham Jail).
17.   Walker, 388 U.S. at 321–22 (1967); GRIFFIN,
supra note 16, at 170–71. *See also* David Luban, *Legal
Storytelling: Difference Made Legal: The Court and King*, 87
MICH. L. REV. 2152 (1989).
18.   RABOTEAU, *supra* note 7, at 110 (emphasis
added). *See also* Randall Kennedy, *Martin Luther King's
Constitution: A Legal History of the Montgomery Bus Boycott*, 98
YALE L.J. 999, 1000 (1989) (describing King's first public speech
as the leader of the Montgomery Bus Boycott as displaying
attentiveness to legal symbolism). Moreover, in recognition of the
interdisciplinary connectedness of law and religion, after King's
death the editors of the *Columbia Law Review* dedicated an issue
to King's life and works. *See generally, Symposium in Memory of
Martin Luther King, Jr.*, 68 COLUM. L. REV. 1011 (1968).
19.   As a point of theological and philosophical
lineage, in King's essay on civil disobedience, *Letter From
Birmingham Jail*, King cites St. Augustine, affectionately
regarded by theologians as the great doctor and teacher of the
church. *See* INVITATION TO CHRISTIAN SPIRITUALITY: AN
ECUMENICAL ANTHOLOGY 103–13 (John R. Tyson ed., 1999)
(highlighting St. Augustine's life and theology). St. Augustine's
teachings are known to have significantly influenced the
theology of King's namesake, Martin Luther, an Augustinian
monk who demonstrated civil disobedience against canon law
after disagreeing with the Catholic Church and posting on the
church door in Wittenberg his famed *Ninety-Five Theses on the
Power and Efficacy of Indulgences*, a point-by-point refutation of
Catholic Church orthodoxy. *See generally*, DAVID M. WHITFORD,
LUTHER: A GUIDE FOR THE PERPLEXED (2011). Indeed, Martin
Luther's protest—an act of civil disobedience by this Article's
definition—began the Protestant Reformation in Germany. *See
generally* GONZÁLEZ *supra* note 12 at 25–31. Moreover, St.
Augustine and Martin Luther, figures King undoubtedly studied
in seminary, were impacted by the Apostle Paul's theology as an

evangelist and apologist in early church history. Although the subject of authentic and disputed ("deutero-Pauline") authorship is beyond this Article's scope [*see, e.g.*, JAIME CLARK-SOLES, ENGAGING THE WORD: THE NEW TESTAMENT AND THE CHRISTIAN BELIEVER 77–87 (2010). *See also* BRUCE J. MALINA & JOHN J. PILCH, SOCIAL SCIENCE COMMENTARY ON THE LETTERS OF PAUL 116–18 (2006)], *Galatians*, a good example, is an epistle scholars uniformly agree Paul actually wrote. *See, e.g.*, MICHAEL J. GORMAN, APOSTLE OF THE CRUCIFIED LORD: A THEOLOGICAL INTRODUCTION TO PAUL & HIS LETTERS 87 (2004). *See also* MARION L. SOARDS, THE APOSTLE PAUL: AN INTRODUCTION TO HIS WRITINGS AND TEACHING 57 (1987) (noting that the theology of agape is omnipresent). In expressing "group love" as a universally shared sentiment among believers, St. Paul, a Pharisaic Israelite, famously penned: "There is no longer Jew or Greek, there is no longer slave or free, there is no longer male and female; for all of you are one in Christ Jesus. And if you belong to Christ, then you are Abraham's offspring, heirs according to the promise." *Galatians* 3:28-29. *See also Philemon* 10–16 (describing Paul's appeal to Philemon to accept Onesimus, Philemon's former slave, back into his household as a "brother" in Christ with Paul as a mutual spiritual father). It is therefore apparent that the theology of agape transcended from apostolic evangelism in antiquity to King in the Movement. *See, e.g.*, MARSH, *supra* note 7, at 45 (quoting King, while pastor of Dexter Avenue Baptist Church in Montgomery, as saying "[s]egregation is a blatant denial of the unity which we all have in Jesus Christ . . . . it is still true that in Christ there is no Jew nor Gentile (Negro nor white) and that out of one blood God made all men to dwell upon the face of the earth.").

20.   PARIS, *supra* note 8, at 79; HOWARD THURMAN, WITH HEAD AND HEART: THE AUTOBIOGRAPHY OF HOWARD THURMAN 113–14 (1979) (discussing his core allegiance to Christianity because of its core principles). *See also* HOWARD THURMAN, JESUS AND THE DISINHERITED 11–35 (1949) (explaining the religion of Jesus Christ as one who was an advocate for the marginalized in society).

21.   King, *Letter from Birmingham Jail*, *supra* note 9, at 78-80.

22.   *Id.*

23.   PARIS, *supra* note 8, at 83. Moreover, consistent
with his biblical beliefs on redemptive suffering, as a disclaimer,
King noted his reluctance to bring attention to his personal trials
because he did not want to be seen as someone with a martyr
complex who was in search of sympathy. MARTIN LUTHER KING,
JR., *Suffering and Faith*, 77 CHRISTIAN CENTURY 510 (1960),
reprinted in A TESTAMENT OF HOPE: THE ESSENTIAL WRITINGS
AND SPEECHES OF MARTIN LUTHER KING, JR. 41 (James M.
Washington ed., 1991) (*"My personal trials have also taught me
the value of unmerited suffering. . . . I have lived these last few
years with the conviction that unearned suffering is redemptive."*)
(internal citations omitted) (emphasis added). *See also*
RABOTEAU, *supra* note 7, at 113 (*"King explained that
nonviolence . . . was based upon the firm conviction that suffering
was redemptive because it could transform both the sufferer and
the oppressor*; it tried to convert, not defeat, the opponent; and it
was based on the confidence that justice would, in the end, win
over injustice."*) (emphasis added). Moreover, the Pauline
Epistles also share this perspective, *see, e.g., Romans* 8:17
("[A]nd if children, heirs also, heirs of God and fellow heirs with
Christ, if indeed we suffer with *Him* in order that we may also be
glorified with *Him*."), as does the oldest gospel narrative, in
showing Jesus came to die for others, *see Mark* 10:45 ("For even
the Son of Man did not come to be served, but to serve, and to
give His life a ransom for many."). Moreover, King's concept of
redemptive suffering was one of the essential faith tenants of the
early Christian Church in believing humankind's debt resulting
from original sin had been paid by Jesus. *See* ST. ATHANASIUS,
ON   THE   INCARNATION   (Cliff   Lee   ed.,   2007),
http://www.ccel.org/ccel/athanasius/incarnation.pdf (last visited
March 11, 2014). *See also* 1 JUSTO L. GONZÁLEZ, THE STORY OF
CHRISTIANITY: THE EARLY CHURCH TO THE DAWN OF THE
REFORMATION 199–201 (2010) (summarizing Athanasius'
Christology as believing the debt of human sin was so significant
that God himself became incarnate in the form of Jesus Christ to
suffer and die for the redemption of humankind such that
believers might not perish but have eternal life); READINGS IN
CHRISTIAN THOUGHT 82–93 (Hugh T. Kerr ed., 2d ed. 1990)
(discussing the theology of Anselm of Canterbury and his belief
that Jesus' incarnation and unmerited redemptive suffering was
to forgive human sin).

THE KEYS ARE BEING PASSED

24.   *See, e.g.,* GLENN TINDER, THE FABRIC OF HOPE: AN ESSAY 71–72 (1999) (explaining the connectedness of hope and suffering through "the concept of justification by faith").

25.   MARTIN LUTHER KING, JR., *Nonviolence and Racial Justice,* 74 CHRISTIAN CENTURY 165 (1957), *reprinted in* A TESTAMENT OF HOPE: THE ESSENTIAL WRITINGS AND SPEECHES OF MARTIN LUTHER KING, JR. 7–9 (James M. Washington ed., 1991) (emphasis added).

26.   Named for the major prophet of Jerusalem and son of Amoz who is believed to be one of the composite's authors, *Isaiah* was written by at least three different people who presumably were prophets during various stages in Israel's history. Indeed, a textual analysis allows the reader to discern three distinct periods, each portrayed in the composite's respective sections. *Isaiah* 1–39, referred to as "First Isaiah," is believed to have been written by the composite's namesake, a prophet of the Southern Kingdom (Judah). Moreover, it is believed to have been written during the time the Southern Kingdom was under Assyrian domination to the Northeast, after the Northern Kingdom (Israel) had ceased to independently exist. The prophet Isaiah presents a message of social justice, faith in God, reward for the obedient, and judgment on the unfaithful. *Isaiah* 40–55, commonly referred to as "Second Isaiah" or "Deutero-Isaiah," is attributed to an unknown prophet who presumably lived in Babylon during the Sixth Century Babylonian exile. A logical deduction is that Second Isaiah's author ministered to the people of Israel during their exile. Consequently, "Deutero-Isaiah" shows continuity with "First Isaiah" by emphasizing trust in God and hope for Israel's imminent return from exile, a period of redemptive suffering. "Second Isaiah" is therefore messianic in providing hopeful anticipation for a redemptive reconciliation after a period of suffering. Finally, *Isaiah* 56–66, attributed to prophet(s) who lived in Judah after Israel's return from exile, is commonly referred to as "Third Isaiah" or "Trito-Isaiah." It is believed to have been written much later than "Second Isaiah." Its similarities with the writings of Haggai and Zechariah suggest "Third Isaiah" was written in the Fourth Century. Moreover, its overall eschatological interest is in events surrounding the last days and on salvation. Accordingly, as a composite, *Isaiah* connects the aforementioned periods of Israel's history and

Jonathan C. Augustine

establishes a theme of messianic salvation and eventual reward after redemptive suffering. *See generally* Geoffrey W. Grogan, *Isaiah*, in 6 THE EXPOSITOR'S BIBLE COMMENTARY 4–13 (Frank E. Gaebelein, gen. ed. 1986). *See also* THE HARPER COLLINS STUDY BIBLE: NEW REVISED AND STANDARD VERSION 1011–13 (Wayne A. Meeks ed., 1993).

     27.   *Isaiah* 53:4–12. The cited pericope demonstrates the sinless suffering of God's servant such that all people might receive salvation. This sinless suffering was arguably the very essence of King's theology. The pericope was written after the fall of Jerusalem in 587 B.C. and during the period of the Babylonian exile before King Cyrus of Persia defeated Babylon in 539 B.C. Consequently, its author(s)' prophesies were directed toward those in exile and were likely delivered shortly before their 538 B.C. return to Judah, as a means of establishing hope. *See* LYNNE M. DEMING, 12 BASIC BIBLE COMMENTARY: ISAIAH 128-32 (1988). Similarly, with respect to the Movement, "hope" fueled the optimism that sustained the Movement's sacrificial activity. *See,* HARDING, *supra* note 1, at 95 (discussing the Student Nonviolent Coordinating Committee's founding statement of purpose: "We affirm the philosophical or religious ideal of nonviolence as the foundation of our purpose, the presupposition of our faith, and the manner of our action. Nonviolence as it grows from Judaic-Christian traditions seeks a social order of justice permeated by love.").

     28.   *See, e.g.,* MICHAEL D. COOGAN, A BRIEF INTRODUCTION TO THE OLD TESTAMENT: THE HEBREW BIBLE IN ITS CONTEXT 334–35 (2009).

     29.   After espousing upon the realities of prison for Blacks during the Movement, including anticipated beatings and the harsh separation from family, King wrote about young people's willingness to suffer in prison as part of the Movement and for the cause in which they believed: "There were no more powerful moments in the Birmingham episode than during the closing days of the campaign, when Negro youngsters ran after white policemen, asking to be locked up. There was an element of unmalicious [sic] mischief in this. The Negro youngsters, although perfectly willing to submit to imprisonment, knew that we had already filled up the jails, and that the police had no place left to take them. When, for decades, you have been able to make a man compromise his manhood by threatening him with a

cruel and unjust punishment, and when suddenly he turns upon you and says: 'Punish me. I do not deserve it. But because I do not deserve it, I will accept it so that the world will know that I am right and you are wrong,' you hardly know what to do. You feel defeated and secretly ashamed. You know that this man is as good a man as you are; that from some mysterious source he has found the courage and the conviction to meet physical force with soul force." Martin Luther King, Jr., *The Sword That Heals*, *in* WHY WE CAN'T WAIT 30 (1968).

    30.   *See Id.* at 2–3 (emphasis added).

    31.   MARTIN LUTHER KING, JR., Love, Law, and Civil Disobedience, Address Before the Fellowship of the Concerned (Nov. 16, 1961), *in* A TESTAMENT OF HOPE: THE ESSENTIAL WRITINGS AND SPEECHES OF MARTIN LUTHER KING, JR., at 52 (James M. Washington ed., 1991) (emphasis added). Many members of the clergy, Black and White, were also engaged in the Freedom Rides. On September 15, 1961, only days before a noted Interstate Commerce Commission ruling, several ordained ministers were singled out by the Hinds County, Mississippi courts to receive punitive fines and sentences of incarceration for their role in the Freedom Rides. *See* RAY ARSENAULT. FREEDOM RIDERS: 1961 AND THE STRUGGLE FOR RACIAL JUSTICE, at 434.

    32.   In detailing the violent beatings the Freedom Riders endured in May 1961 and their suffering servant resilience, author Helene Hanff observes: "[t]he riders stayed in Montgomery four days, as guests in Negro homes, until the injured among them were able to travel. On Wednesday, May 24, accompanied by National Guardsmen and sixteen reporters, they left Montgomery for Jackson, with James Lawson holding classes on nonviolent techniques on the bus as it rode into Mississippi. At Jackson, twenty-seven Freedom Riders were arrested and given the choice of a two hundred dollar fine or two months in jail. Since fines were an enormous burden, the students chose jail. They were immediately transferred from the city jail to Parchman State Penitentiary. There, nine black girls were locked in one filthy cell with the white girls occupying an adjoining cell. The cells contained nothing but mattresses and sheets thrown on the steel floor. When the girls began to sing freedom songs, prison guards took their mattresses away. When they sang the Star-Spangled Banner the guards took their sheets away. For three nights, they slept on the steel floor." HELENE

Jonathan C. Augustine

HANFF, THE MOVERS AND SHAKERS: THE YOUNG ACTIVISTS OF THE
SIXTIES, at 32 (1970).
    33.   *See* JOSEPH, *supra* note 3, at 125–126.
    34.   *Id.* at 126.
    35.   ANTHONY LEWIS, FREEDOM FOR THE THOUGHT
THAT WE HATE: A BIOGRAPHY OF THE FIRST AMENDMENT, at ix–x
(2007).
    36.   William F. Buckley, Jr., *Separation of Church
and State of a Different Kind*, HOUSTON CHRON., Mar. 23, 2006, at
B11, *available at*
http://www.chron.com/opinion/outlook/article/Buckley-Separation-
of-church-and-state-of-a-1499414.php (defending Catholic
Cardinal Roger Mahoney of Los Angeles in a decision to ask
Catholics to deliberately disobey an immigration law the U.S.
Conference of Catholic Bishops deemed immoral) (last visited
March 11, 2014).
    37.   *See, e.g.*, Matthew R. Hall, *Guilty But Civilly
Disobedient: Reconciling Civil Disobedience and the Rule of Law*,
28 CARDOZO L. REV. 2083, 2085 n.2 (2007); Steven M. Bauer &
Peter J. Eckerstrom, Note, *The State Made Me Do It: The
Applicability of the Necessity Defense to Civil Disobedience*, 39
STAN. L. REV. 1173, 1175 n.14 (1987); Symposium, *Symposium
on Civil Disobedience*, 5 NOTRE DAME J. L. ETHICS & PUB. POL'Y
(1991).
    38.   *See* Henry David Thoreau, *Civil Disobedience, in*
THE POWER OF NONVIOLENCE 15 (2002).
    39.   *See, e.g.*, GARROW, BEARING THE CROSS, *supra*
note 2, 127-72 (discussing the North Carolina A&T college
students' February 1, 1960, sit-ins in protest of racial
segregation laws at the F.W. Woolworth lunch counter in
Greensboro, N.C., along with Dr. King's vocal support of the
college students' activities); DOROTHY STERLING, TEAR DOWN THE
WALLS!: A HISTORY OF THE AMERICAN CIVIL RIGHTS MOVEMENT
190–93 (1968). Moreover, there are also countless historical
examples of how interfaith clergy and seminarians hosted and
participated in public demonstrations against unjust laws. *See,
e.g.*, TAYLOR BRANCH, AT CANAAN'S EDGE: AMERICA IN THE KING
YEARS 1965–68, at 216–17 (2006).
    40.   *See* U.S. CONST. amend. I. *See also* Gregory A.
Mark, *The Vestigial Constitution: The History and Significance of
the Right to Petition*, 66 FORDHAM L. REV. 2153 (1998) (providing a

historical analysis of the First Amendment's Petition Clause, with an emphasis on its political origins in colonial America, and discussing its inherently political function); Julie M. Spanbauer, *The First Amendment Right to Petition Government for a Redress of Grievances: Cut From a Different Cloth*, 21 HASTINGS CONST. L.Q. 15 (1993). Although the First Amendment concept of petitioning government for redress of grievances can mean an indirect petition through Congress, as other scholarship makes clear, it was not until after the VRA's 1965 enactment that there was a significant increase in the number of African Americans elected to Congress and to state legislatures. *See, e.g.*, Jonathan C. Augustine, *Rethinking Shaw v. Reno, The Supreme Court's Benign Race-Related Jurisprudence and Louisiana's Recent Reapportionment: The Argument for Intermediate Scrutiny in Racial Gerrymandering According to the Voting Rights Act*, 29 S.U. L. REV. 151, 151-52 (2002). Indeed, there was no Congressional Black Caucus as is known today. *See*, CBC, "about" http://cbc.fudge.house.gov/about/ (last visited March 11, 2014). During the Movement, therefore, even though the First Amendment's right to petition included political participation, prior to the VRA's enactment, the track of civil challenge was limited to the petitioning of government through the judicial system.

    41.   The oft-cited *Brown v. Board of Education.*, 347 U.S. 483 (1954), challenging the constitutionality of school segregation laws under the Fourteenth Amendment's Equal Protection Clause, provides an example of civil challenge. *See, e.g.*, ROBERT J. COTTROL, RAYMOND T. DIAMOND & LELAND B. WARE, *BROWN V. BOARD OF EDUCATION*: CASTE, CULTURE, AND THE CONSTITUTION 101–18 (2003) (detailing the NAACP's many efforts at challenging "separate but equal" in public education); RAWN JAMES, JR., ROOT AND BRANCH: CHARLES HAMILTON HOUSTON, THURGOOD MARSHALL, AND THE STRUGGLE TO END SEGREGATION (2010); CHARLES J. OGLETREE, JR., ALL DELIBERATE SPEED: REFLECTIONS ON THE FIRST HALF CENTURY OF *BROWN V. BOARD OF EDUCATION*, 116–23 (2004) (discussing Charles Hamilton Houston's role as special counsel to the NAACP and the many litigious challenges instituted against Jim Crow segregation laws); Jonathan C. Augustine & Craig M. Freeman, *Grading the Graders and Reforming the Reform: An Analysis of the State of Public Education Ten Years After No*

Child Left Behind, 57 LOY. L. REV. 237, 264–67 (2011) (discussing many of the systemic inequities in public educational systems resulting from de jure and de facto segregation). *See also*, Wendy B. Scott, *Dr. King and Parents Involved: The Battle for Hearts and Minds*, 32 N.Y.U. REV. L. & SOC. CHANGE 543 (2008).

42.   During the Montgomery Bus Boycott, an act that resulted from Parks's act of civil disobedience, members of the Montgomery Improvement Association concurrently engaged in civil challenge by testing the constitutionality of an Alabama state statute and companion Montgomery municipal ordinance requiring racial segregation in carriers of public transportation. The Alabama federal district court declared the laws unconstitutional and the United States Supreme Court affirmed on appeal. *Browder v. Gayle*, 142 F. Supp. 707, 715-17 (M.D. Al. 1956), *aff'd*, 352 U.S. 903 (1956) (distinguishing *Plessy v. Ferguson*, 163 U.S. 537 (1896) and relying on *Shelley v. Kramer*, 334 U.S. 1, 22 (1948) to declare the Alabama laws at issue unconstitutional).

43.   *See* generally, *Cox v. Louisiana*, 379 U.S. 536 (1965) (reversing the state court convictions of Rev. B. Elton Cox for his leadership in a peaceful assembly protesting segregation and discriminatory practices in downtown Baton Rouge, Louisiana).

44.   *See* generally, *Shuttlesworth v. City of Birmingham*, 394 U.S. 147 (1969); *Edwards v. South Carolina*, 372 U.S. 229 (1963).

45.   *See, e.g., Brown v. Louisiana*, 383 U.S. 131 (1966).

46.   *See, e.g., Louisiana ex rel. Gremillion v. NAACP*, 366 U.S. 293 (1961).

47.   *See, e.g., N. Y. Times Co. v. Sullivan*, 376 U.S. 254 (1964) (redefining the legal concept of libel under the First Amendment); *Gremillion*, 366 U.S. 293 (detailing freedom of association); Kennedy, *supra* note 18, at 1001, 1012.

48.   Kennedy, *supra* note18, at 1001 (internal citations omitted). It bears noting that during the Movement, the Court was also required to give expansive breadth to the First Amendment because of the conscience protest by non-clergy, as well. *See, e.g., Cohen v. California*, 403 U.S. 15 (1971) (holding that the First Amendment's guarantee of free speech covered the

wearing of a jacket with the inscription "Fuck the Draft" while in a government building).
    49.   *See, e.g., Cox v. Louisiana*, 379 U.S. 536 (1965) (discussed *infra* at note 56).
    50.   King was arrested in Birmingham, Alabama (on Good Friday, April 12, 1963) where he penned the famous *Letter From a Birmingham Jail* in response to other members of the clergy that criticized his actions as "unwise and untimely." King's arrest was for defying a state court injunction barring peaceful assembly, a right he understood the First Amendment guaranteed. Martin Luther King, Jr., *Civil Disobedience Should Be Employed, in* THE CIVIL RIGHTS MOVEMENT: OPPOSING VIEWPOINTS 116, 122–23 (William Dudley ed., 1996). Professor Paris also writes the following, explaining the basis for King's civil disobedience: "Martin Luther King's respect for the law is well known. He constantly sought to convince his followers that nonviolent direct action did not imply any disrespect for the just laws of the land, inasmuch as it was always practiced for the sake of legal justice. Further, the method is justified by the American Constitution, which provides for legal protest as the means for the redress of grievances. King opposed all forms of anarchy with a passion similar to that with which he opposed tyranny. Since he considered the fundamental problem in America to be the moral cleavage between the national practice and the law of the cosmos, and since the civil rights movement was intended to be the agent for moral reform, he advocated a method for that reform that he could justify by an appeal to the moral law of the universe. He deemed it significant that the Constitution was a document that described truths in accord with that moral law. However, he viewed the nation's customs and practices as contradictions of that law, and consequently, he had no difficulty in appealing to the Constitution as a source for justifying many of his actions since that law was commensurate with the universal moral law." PARIS, *supra* note 8, at 86–87.
    51.   Martin Luther King, Jr., *Speech at Holt Street Baptist Church in Montgomery, Alabama on December 5, 1955, in* THE EYES ON THE PRIZE CIVIL RIGHTS READER: DOCUMENTS, SPEECHES, AND FIRSTHAND ACCOUNTS FROM THE BLACK FREEDOM STRUGGLE 48, 49 (Clayborne Carson et al. eds., 1991) (emphasis added) (speaking at Holt Street Baptist Church in Montgomery, Alabama on December 5, 1955). *See also* Kennedy, *supra* note 18,

at 1000–01. King spoke about the "right to protest for right" while addressing the illegality of court-issued injunctions prohibiting civil rights activists from exercising the constitutionally guaranteed rights of free speech and free association. The occasion was King's last public address on April 3, 1968, the evening before his assassination. King and members of the Movement were in Memphis, Tennessee in support of the city's sanitation workers' strike for better wages. In relevant part, King remarked: "Now about injunctions: We have an injunction and we're going into court tomorrow morning to fight this illegal, unconstitutional injunction. All we say to America is 'Be true to what you said on paper.' If I lived in China or even Russia, or any totalitarian country, maybe I could understand the denial of certain basic First Amendment privileges, because they hadn't committed themselves to that over there. But somewhere I read of the freedom of assembly. Somewhere I read of the freedom of speech. Somewhere I read of the freedom of the press. Somewhere I read that the greatness of America is the right to protest for right. And so I say, we aren't going to let an injunction turn us around. We are going on." Martin Luther King, Jr., *Speech at the Mason Temple in Memphis, Tennessee on April 3, 1968, in* THE EYES ON THE PRIZE CIVIL RIGHTS READER: DOCUMENTS, SPEECHES, AND FIRSTHAND ACCOUNTS FROM THE BLACK FREEDOM STRUGGLE 409, 413 (Clayborne Carson et al. eds., 1991) (speaking at the Mason Temple in Memphis, Tennessee on April 3, 1968).

     52.   JOHN E. NOWAK & RONALD D. ROTUNDA, CONSTITUTIONAL LAW 1146 (7th ed. 2004).

     53.   ANDREW P. NAPOLITANO, THE CONSTITUTION IN EXILE 19 (2006). Further, relevant to the First Amendment challenges during the Movement is the fact that although the Bill of Rights originally only applied to the federal government, it was made applicable to the states through the Fourteenth Amendment's Due Process Clause. *See, e.g.,* Everson v. Bd. of Educ., 330 U.S. 1 (1947); Akhil Reed Amir, *The Bill of Rights and Fourteenth Amendment,* 101 YALE L.J. 1193 (1992) (discussing various theories of incorporation).

     54.   *See, e.g.,* GOODWIN LIU, PAMELA S. KARLAN & CHRISTOPHER H. SCHROEDER, KEEPING FAITH WITH THE CONSTITUTION 15 (2009). Arguably, there is no constitutional

limitation on governmental authority more clear than the express limitations imposed by the First Amendment.

55.   *Brown v. Louisiana*, 383 U.S. 131 (1966).

56.   *Id.* at 133. In the other three cases, *Garner v. Louisiana*, 368 U.S. 157 (1961), *Taylor v. Louisiana*, 370 U.S. 154 (1962), and *Cox v. Louisiana*, 379 U.S. 536 (1965), all of the civil rights protestors were found guilty of violating Louisiana's then-existing breach of the peace statute for their public protests of discriminatory laws. In *Cox*, for example, Rev. Cox, an ordained Congregational minister, led a peaceful protest in front of the courthouse in Baton Rouge, the state's capitol. *Cox*, 379 U.S. at 541–42. In all three of the previous cases, the demonstrators' state court convictions were overturned. *Brown*, 383 U.S. at 133. In *Brown*, however, the Court took special consideration of the case's factual history because it involved a quasi-public protest within the parameters of a closed-door public library. *Brown*, 383 U.S. at 135.

57.   *Brown*, 383 U.S. at 141–43. The *Brown* opinion was written by Associate Justice Fortas. He was joined by Chief Justice Warren and Associate Justice Douglas. The opinion reached by the three-justice plurality received majority support in the form of two separately written concurrences by Associate Justices Brennan and White. The Court's four-member dissent included Associate Justices Black, Clark, Harlan, and Stewart.

58.   *Id.* at 135–36.

59.   *Id.* at 138.

60.   *Id.* at 141–42 (internal citations omitted).

61.   *See Id.* Moreover, in addressing the related Fourteenth Amendment Equal Protection Clause issue of the discriminatory use of public libraries, the Court wrote that "[a] State or its instrumentality may, of course, regulate the use of its libraries or other public facilities. But it must do so in a reasonable and nondiscriminatory manner, equally applicable to all and administered with equality to all." *Id.* at 143.

62.   *Edwards v. South Carolina*, 372 U.S. 229 (1963).

63.   *Id.* at 238.

64.   *Id.* at 229–30.

65.   *Id.*

66.   *Id.* Such a "petitioning" of government for redress of grievances was clearly political in nature and

presumably the type of express protection the Framers intended to include in the First Amendment.

67.   *Edwards*, 372 U.S. at 233.

68.   *Id.* (internal citations omitted).

69.   *Id.* at 234.

70.   *Id.* at 235.

71.   *Id.* at 235–36 (internal citations omitted).

72.   *Id.* at 237–38 (quoting *Terminiello v. Chicago*, 337 U.S. 1, 4–5 (1949)). Similarly, in *NAACP v. Alabama ex rel. Patterson*, 357 U.S. 449 (1958), the Supreme Court vacated an Alabama state court disclosure order requiring the state NAACP branch to produce lists of all its members as an unconstitutional violation of the Fourteenth Amendment's Due Process Clause. *Id.* at 466. In so doing, the Court focused on the First Amendment's rights of association and expression. *Id.* at 460–64. *See also, NAACP v. Button*, 371 U.S. 415, 428–29 (1963) (reversing the Virginia Supreme Court of Appeals' injunction against the Virginia NAACP Branch's legal operations as an unconstitutional violation of the First and Fourteenth Amendments).

73.   *Edwards*, 372 U.S. at 238. *See also* ANN FAGAN GINGER, THE LAW, THE SUPREME COURT, AND THE PEOPLE'S RIGHTS 29–36 (1977) (describing the significance of the *Edwards* Court's ruling).

74.   In relevant part, the Commerce Clause of the United States Constitution provides that "Congress shall have the power to . . . regulate Commerce with foreign Nations, and among the several States, and with the Indian Tribes." U.S. CONST. art. I, § 8, cl. 3.

75.   *Morgan v. Virginia*, 328 U.S. 373, 385–86 (1946).

76.   *Boynton v. Virginia*, 364 U.S. 454, 459–60 (1960) (overturning the conviction of an African American law student for trespassing because he was in a segregated restaurant in a bus terminal and declaring that such discriminatory practices violated the Interstate Commerce Act of 1887, as amended).

77.   49 C.F.R. 180a (1963). *See also, United States v. City of Jackson*, 318 F.2d 1 (5th Cir. 1963); *Freedom Fighters: Freedom to Travel*, PBS: http://www.pbs.org/wgbh/americanexperience/freedomriders/issues/freedom-to-travel (last visited March 11, 2014).

78. 49 C.F.R. 180a (1963). *See also* ARSENAULT, *supra* note 31, at 439–41. After the Interstate Commerce Commission issued a unanimous eleven member ruling, beginning November 1, 1961, all interstate carriers "would be required to display a certificate that read 'Seating aboard this vehicle is without regard to race, color, creed, or national origin, by order of the Interstate Commerce Commission.'" *Id.* at 439.

79. Before the controversial and judicially decided 2000 presidential election, the 1960 election was reputed to be the closest in American history. *See, e.g.*, CHRISTOPHER MATTHEWS, KENNEDY & NIXON: THE RIVALRY THAT SHAPED POSTWAR AMERICA 170–80 (1996). In explaining part of the African American community's new allegiance to then-Senator Kennedy in the 1960 election, sociology scholar Antoine Joseph posits: "A strong argument can be made that John F. Kennedy owed his election in 1960 to the phone calls he made to Coretta Scott King. His phone calls received wide publicity in the black press, but were virtually ignored by the white media. Kennedy was the beneficiary of a dramatic shift in the black vote. In 1956, Blacks had voted Republican by a 60-to-40 margin, but in the 1960 election they voted Democrat by a 70-to-30 margin. The campaign's clever usage of Kennedy's concern for the jailed Martin Luther King stimulated black turnout, while the white press's neglectfulness prevented a backlash. JOSEPH, *supra* note 3, at 122. *See also* MARTIN LUTHER KING, JR., *Atlanta Arrest and Presidential Politics, in* THE AUTOBIOGRAPHY OF MARTIN LUTHER KING, JR. 144–50 (Clayborne Carson ed., 1998).

80. *See* DAVID J. GARROW, PROTEST AT SELMA: MARTIN LUTHER KING, JR. AND THE VOTING RIGHTS ACT OF 1965 xi (1979) at 73–77. On Bloody Sunday, uniformed officers brutally beat clergy and unarmed laity. BRANCH, *supra* note 39, at 54–55. As historian Taylor Branch writes: "Doctors and nurses worked feverishly through more than a hundred patients, bandaging heads, daubing eyes, shipping more serious cases to the only local hospital that would treat them—Good Samaritan, a Catholic mission facility run by the Edmundite Order in a Negro neighborhood. . . . Lafayette Surney found John Lewis at Good Samaritan two hours after the rampage, admitted for a fractured skull. FBI agents reported the most common injuries to be lacerations and broken bones, but Lewis and Surney alike saw

more suffering from tear gas that still seeped out of the patients' saturated clothes." *Id.*
81. BRANCH, *supra* note 39, at xi.
82. Civil Rights Act of 1964, Pub. L. No. 88-352, 78 Stat. 241 (codified in scattered sections of 42 U.S.C.).
83. *See, e.g.,* Jonathan C. Augustine & Hon. Ulysses Gene Thibodeaux, *Forty Years Later: Chronicling the Voting Rights Act of 1965 and Its Impact on Louisiana's Judiciary,* 66 LA. L. REV. 453, 453–94 (2006) (detailing the significant increase in the number of African American lawyers elected to the bench in the state of Louisiana under the VRA and litigation filed pursuant thereto). *See also* ALEX POINSETT, WALKING WITH PRESIDENTS: LOUIS MARTIN AND THE RISE OF BLACK POLITICAL POWER 150–53 (1997) (discussing the advances many African Americans were able to make after the VRA became law, especially through lawsuits in southern states including Mississippi, Louisiana, and Alabama). Furthermore, in also discussing the VRA as the Movement's measure of success, Professor Garrow writes that "[t]he Voting Rights Act of 1965 revolutionized Black access to the ballot throughout most of the Deep South. In so doing, it changed forever the politics of those states and, indirectly, those of the entire nation." GARROW, PROTEST AT SELMA, *supra* note 80, at 1. *See also* Adam B. Cox & Thomas J. Miles, *Judging the Voting Rights Act,* 108 COLUMBIA L. REV. 1, 2 (2008) ("The Voting Rights Act has dramatically reshaped the political landscape of the United States. In the four decades since its enactment, it has helped substantially expand political opportunities for minority voters and has contributed to the radical realignment of southern politics").
84. ANDREW YOUNG, AN EASY BURDEN: THE CIVIL RIGHTS MOVEMENT AND THE TRANSFORMATION OF AMERICA 326 (1996). Both the Civil Rights Act of 1964 and Voting Rights Act of 1965 were upheld as valid congressional enactments after judicial challenge before the United States Supreme Court. *See, e.g., South Carolina v. Katzenbach,* 383 U.S. 301 (1966) (upholding challenged provisions of the Voting Rights Act as constitutional); *Heart of Atlanta Motel, Inc. v. United States,* 379 U.S. 241 (1964) (upholding as valid the public accommodations provisions of the Civil Rights Act of 1964).
85. Notwithstanding the Civil Rights Acts of 1957 and 1960, as Professor Garrow writes in addressing the voting

demographics in Alabama's Dallas County in April 1961 "Blacks comprised approximately half of the voting-age population of Dallas County, within which Selma was situated, but only 156 of them, out of 15,000 or so, were registered voters, and only fourteen had been added to the rolls since 1954." GARROW, PROTEST AT SELMA, *supra* note 80, at 31.

86. *See, e.g., United States v. Mississippi,* 380 U.S. 128 (1965); *Gomillion v. Lightfoot,* 364 U.S. 339 (1960); *Baker v. Carr,* 369 U.S. 186 (1962).

87. Tricia Ann Martinez, Comment, *When Appearance Matters: Reapportionment Under the Voting Rights Act and* Shaw v. Reno, 54 LA. L. REV. 1335, 1336 (1994). Moreover, as Kennedy chronicles, "[a]lthough the Fifteenth Amendment to the Constitution prohibited states from disenfranchising persons on account of race, the White South openly and successfully used private power and state authority to deny the Negro the ballot." Kennedy, *supra* note 18, at 1006 (internal citations omitted).

88. *See, e.g., City of Richmond v. J.A. Croson Co.,* 488 U.S. 469, 521–22 (1989) (noting that Section 5 of the Fourteenth Amendment gives Congress the unique power to combat state existent problems of race) (Scalia, J., concurring). Moreover, as the Supreme Court noted the year prior to the Act's passage, "[u]ndoubtedly, the right of suffrage is a fundamental matter in a free and democratic society." *Reynolds v. Sims,* 377 U.S. 533, 561–62 (1964).

89. Augustine & Thibodeaux, *supra* note 83, at 453–54. African Americans were originally granted the right to vote during Reconstruction, with Amendment XV to the United States Constitution ("the Fifteenth Amendment"). In relevant part, the Fifteenth Amendment provides that "[t]he right of citizens of the United States to vote shall not be denied or abridged by the United States or by any State on account of race, color, or previous condition of servitude." U.S. CONST. amend. XV, § 1.

90. The Fifteenth Amendment expressly provides that "Congress shall have the power to enforce this article by appropriate legislation." U.S. CONST. amend. XV, §2.

91. *See* POINSETT, *supra* note 83, at 153. With respect to the VRA's enactment and immediate effects: The Voting Rights Act included: (1) the prohibition of literacy tests

and similar voting restrictions; (2) the empowerment of the attorney general to oversee federal elections in seven southern states by appointing examiners to register those denied the right to vote; and (3) instructions to the attorney general to challenge the constitutionality of poll taxes in state and local elections. JOSEPH, *supra* note 3, at 126.

92.   *See generally*, Augustine, *supra* note 40, at 152 (discussing the election of several African Americans to the United States House of Representatives in congressional districts drawn under the VRA); Robert B. McDuff, *Judicial Elections and the Voting Rights Act*, 38 LOY. L. REV. 931, 939–45 (1993) (detailing VRA cases in which he served as lead counsel with the Lawyers' Committee for Civil Rights Under Law that extended the Act to the elected judiciary). *See also* GARROW, PROTEST AT SELMA, *supra* note 80, at xi. Further, in discussing the VRA's significance, while also describing his then-work as an attorney with President Johnson's Office of Economic Opportunity ("OEO") and associated work with the non-profit Voter Education Project ("VEP"), civil rights icon Vernon Jordan writes: "[T]he passage of the Voting Rights Act in August 1965 changed the entire landscape. For the first time, federal registrars came to the South to make sure that local officials did not thwart the enforcement of the law. From my office at the OEO, I understood immediately what this might mean: The VEP could now do better at the job it had been designed to do. With the help and protection of the federal government, money from this not-for-profit entity could be used to transform the Southern electorate and, along with it, the South." VERNON E. JORDAN, JR. & ANNETTE GORDON-REED, VERNON CAN READ! A MEMOIR 179 (2001).

93.   *See, e.g.*, National Conference of State Legislatures, REDISTRICTING LAW 2000 47 (NCSL 1999), *available at* http://www.senate.leg.state.mn.us/departments/scr/redist/red2000/c h2equal.htm (last visited March 11, 2014) [hereinafter NCSL]; April D. Dulaney, Comment, *A Judicial Exception for Judicial Elections: "A Burning Scar on the Flesh of the Voting Rights Act,"* 65 TUL. L. REV. 1223, 1223–24 (1991); M. David Gelfand, *Voting Rights and the Democratic Process: Ongoing Struggles and Continuing Questions*, 17 URB. L. 333, 333–34 & n.3 (1985).

94.   NCSL, *supra* note 93, at 47–48 (quoting 42 U.S.C. § 1973 (a)). The vast majority of section 2 claims address challenges to multi-member governmental bodies like city councils, schools boards, county commissions, and state legislatures. Kristen Clarke, *The Obama Factor: The Impact of the 2008 Presidential Election on Future Voting Rights Litigation*, 3 HARV. L. & POL'Y REV. 59, 62 (2009).

95.   *See, South Carolina v. Katzenbach*, 383 U.S. 301, 315 (1966).

96.   *See*, Augustine & Thibodeaux, *supra* note 83, at 459.

97.   *See* NCSL, *supra* note 93, at 48. Moreover, when the VRA was passed, "Section 5 was considered one of the primary enforcement mechanisms to ensure that minority voters would have an opportunity to register to vote and fully participate in the electoral process free of discrimination." NCSL at 80.

98.   "Before passage of section 5, only 29 percent of Blacks were registered to vote in Alabama, Georgia, Louisiana, Mississippi, North Carolina, South Carolina, and Virginia, compared to 73.4 percent of [w]hites. In Mississippi, only 6.7 percent of [b]lacks were registered. By 1967 . . . more than 52 percent of [b]lacks were registered to vote in these states." NCSL at 80 n.345 (internal citations omitted).

99.   Tricia Ann Martinez, Comment, *When Appearance Matters: Reapportionment Under the Voting Rights Act and* Shaw v. Reno, 54 La. L. Rev. 1335 (1994).

100.   *See, e.g., City of Richmond v. J.A. Croson Co.*, 488 U.S. 469, 521–22, 109 S. Ct. 706, 736–37 (1989) (noting that Section five of the Fourteenth Amendment gives Congress the unique power to combat state existent problems of race) (Scalia, J., concurring).

101.   307 U.S. 268, 59 S. Ct. 872 (1939).

102.   *Id.* at 275, 59 S. Ct. at 876.

103.   EDWARD S. CORWIN & J.W. PELTASON, UNDERSTANDING THE CONSTITUTION (4th ed.) (Holt, Rinehart & Winston 1967), at 152.

104.   National Conference of State Legislatures: Redistricting Law 2000, Chpt. 4, *"Racial and Ethnic Discrimination,"* 47 (1999) (hereinafter "NCSL").

105.   See, Reynolds v. Sims, 377 U.S. 533, 561–62, 84 S. Ct. 1362, 1381–82 (1964) ("Undoubtedly, the right of suffrage is a fundamental matter in a free and democratic society."); See also Jonathan C. Augustine, Rethinking Shaw v. Reno, the Supreme Court's Benign Race-Related Jurisprudence and Louisiana's Recent Reapportionment: the Argument for Intermediate Scrutiny in Racial Gerrymandering According to the Voting Rights Act, 29 S.U. L. Rev. 151, 164 (2001–2002); Thurgood Marshall, Reflections on the Bicentennial of the United States Constitution, 101 Harv. L. Rev. 1 (1987–1988).

106.   Tricia Ann Martinez, supra note 99, at 1337.

107.   April D. Dulaney, Comment, A Judicial Exception for Judicial Elections: "A Burning Scar on the Flesh of the Voting Rights Act," 65 Tul. L. Rev. 1223, 1223–24 (1991) (citing David Gelfand, Voting Rights and the Democratic Process: Ongoing Struggles and Continuing Questions, 17 Urb. Law 333, 333–34 & n.3 (1985)).

108.   446 U.S. 55, 100 S. Ct. 1519 (1980). "Congress seized the opportunity to re-examine the entire Voting Rights Act. April D. Dulaney, Comment, A Judicial Exception for Judicial Elections: "A Burning Scar on the Flesh of the Voting Rights Act," 65 Tul. L. Rev. 1223, 1226 (1991) (internal citation omitted). Several members of Congress voiced displeasure regarding the Supreme Court's decision in City of Mobile v. Bolden."

109.   Id. at 62, 100 S. Ct. 1497.

110.   Dulaney, supra note 108, at 1225–26 (internal citations omitted).

111.   Samuel Issacharoff, Polarized Voting and the Political Process: the Transformation of Voting Rights Jurisprudence, 90 Mich. L. Rev. 1833, 1845-46 (1992) (internal citations omitted).

112.   See NCSL, supra note 104, at 48. Congressional response to Bolden was swift. A House Judiciary Committee's report found the intent standard inappropriate and indicated the proper judicial focus should be on election outcomes, not discriminatory intent. See H.R. Rep. No. 227, 97th Cong., 1st Sess. 29–31 (1981).

113.   Chisom v. Edwards, 839 F.2d 1056, 1059. Congress' final adoption of the "results test" included recommendations from the Senate Judiciary Committee,

encompassing relevant language from *White v. Regester*, 412 U.S. 755, 93 S. Ct. 2332 (1973), a case involving multimember state legislative districts in Texas. *See* NCSL, *supra* note 104, at 52.

114.   Issacharoff, *supra* note 111, at 1846 (citations omitted).

115.   NCSL, *supra* note 104, at 53.

116.   S. Rep. No. 417, 97th Cong., 2nd Sess. 16 (1982).

117.   485 F.2d 1297 (5th Cir. 1973) (en banc), aff'd per curiam sub nom., *East Carroll Parish School Board v. Marshall*, 424 U.S. 636, 96 S. Ct. 1083 (1976).

118.   The list of factors included the following: (1) the extent of any history of official discrimination in the state or political subdivision that touched the right of the members of the minority group to register, to vote, or otherwise to participate in the democratic process; (2) the extent to which voting in the election of the state or political subdivision is racially polarized; (3) the extent to which the state or political subdivision has used unusually large election districts, majority vote requirements, anti-single shot provisions, or other voting practice or procedure that may enhance the opportunity for discrimination against the minority group; (4) if there is a candidate slating process, whether the members of the minority group have been denied access to that process; (5) the extent to which members of the minority group in the state or political subdivision bear the effects of discrimination in such areas as education, employment and health, which hinder their ability to participate effectively in the political process; (6) whether political campaigns have been characterized by overt or subtle racial appeals; and (7) the extent to which members of the minority group have been elected to public office in the jurisdiction. *See,* S. Rep. No. 417, 97th Cong. 2nd Sess. 29 (1982); *see also, White v. Regester*, 412 U.S. 755, 765–70, 93 S. Ct. 2332, 2339–42 (1973).

119.   42 U.S.C. § 1973 (b) (1982).

120.   *See,* Robert B. McDuff, *Judicial Elections and the Voting Rights Act*, 38 Loy. L. Rev. 931, 937-38 (1993) (discussing Martin v. Allain, 658 F.Supp. 1183 (S.D. Miss. 1987)).

121.   *See, e.g., United States v. Marengo County Commission*, 731 F.2d 1546 (11th Cir. 1984); *Jones v. City of Lubbock*, 727 F.2d 364 (5th Cir. 1984); *Ketchum v. Byrne*, 740 F.2d 1398 (7th Cir. 1984); *see also, Rybicki v. State Bd. of*

Elections, 574 F. Supp. 1082 (N.D. Ill. 1982) (*Rybicki I*); 574 F. Supp. 1147 (N.D. Ill. 1983) (*Rybicki II*).

122. 478 U.S. 30, 106 S. Ct. 2752 (1986).

123. *Id.* at 44, 106 S. Ct. at 2762–63 (citing S. Rep. No. 417, 97th Cong. 2nd Sess. at 28)

124. *Id.*, 106 S. Ct. at 2762–63; *see also,* McDuff *supra* note 120, at 972 ("The statement in *Gingles* regarding size and compactness of the minority population illustrates one of the requirements in section 2 cases—plaintiffs must demonstrate the potential of creating some other remedial electoral configuration that will improve minority opportunities to elect candidates of choice.").

125. *South Carolina v. Katzenbach,* 383 U.S. 301, 313, 86 S. Ct. 803, 810–11 (1966).

126. NCSL, *supra* note 104, at 80. Before passage of Section 5, only 29 percent of blacks were registered to vote in several southern states, including Louisiana and Mississippi, compared with 73.4 percent of whites. By 1967, only two years after Section 5 was adopted, more than 52 percent of blacks were registered in those same states. *See Id.* (citing B. Grofman, L. Handley, & R. Neimi, Minority Representation and the Quest for Voting Equality 23 (Cambridge University Press 1992)).

127. *See* 425 U.S. 130, 137; 96 S. Ct. 1357, 1361-62 (1976). Even before the Department of Justice rejected the City's Plan I, it began working on Plan II. Plan II was nevertheless also rejected by the attorney general. *See Id.* See 28 C.F.R. § 51.54(a) (2005) for the standard the Department of Justice employs in such cases.

128. *Beer v. United States,* 425 U.S. 130, 143; 96 S. Ct. 1357, 1364 (1976)

129. *Id.* at 138, 96 S. Ct. 1362 (citations omitted) (emphasis added).

130. *Id.* at 141, 96 S. Ct. 1364

131. 460 U.S. 125, 103 S. Ct. 998 (1983).

132. *Id.* at 135, 103 S. Ct. at 1004.

133. *Id.* at 134, 103 S. Ct. at 1004.

134. 520 U.S. 273, 117 S. Ct. 1228 (1997).

135. *Young* at 276, 117 S. Ct. 1232 (citing *Beer v. United States,* 425 U.S. 130, 141, 96 S. Ct. 1357, 1363–64 (1976))

136. *Young* at 290–91, 117 S. Ct. at 1239 (internal citations omitted).

THE KEYS ARE BEING PASSED

137.   *Young* at 291, 117 S. Ct. at 1239.
138.   *See* Augustine & Thibodeaux, *supra* note 83, at 459.
139.   *See* Gerald Gill, *Power!: 1966–1968*, *in* THE EYES ON THE PRIZE CIVIL RIGHTS READER: DOCUMENTS, SPEECHES, AND FIRSTHAND ACCOUNTS FROM THE BLACK FREEDOM STRUGGLE 334 (Clayborne Carson et al., eds., 1991).
140.   *Id.* at 334–35.
141.   *See* Augustine & Thibodeaux, *supra* note 83, at 488–89, n.210 (internal citations omitted).
142.   *See* Gill, *supra* note 139, at 337 (describing the first-ever elections of Blacks to municipal offices).
143.   After conducting what was arguably its most intensive fact-finding, Congress passed the Fannie Lou Hamer, Rosa Parks and Coretta Scott King Voting Rights Reauthorization and Amendments Act of 2006. *See* Jim Sensenbrenner, Fannie Lou Hamer, Rosa Parks, and Coretta Scott King Voting Rights Act Reauthorization and Amendments Act of 2006, H.R. REP. NO. 109–478, 5 (2006); 152nd CONG. REC. S7949, S7967-S7968 (daily ed. July 20, 2006). Before reauthorizing the VRA, the House and Senate Judiciary Committees held congressional hearings between October 18, 2005 and July 13, 2006. *Id.*
144.   Nw. Mun.Util. Dist. No. 1 v. Holder, 129 S.Ct. 2504 (2009).
145.   *Holder*, 129 S.Ct. 2504, 2508.
146.   To be eligible for Section 4's bailout, the interested political entity must seek declaratory relief before a three-judge panel of the United States District Court for the District of Columbia. 42 U.S.C. §§ 1973b (a)(1); 1973c(a). Among other things, the entity must show it has not been found liable of voting rights violations. *See generally,* 42 U.S.C. §§ 1973b(a)(1)(A)–(F).
147.   *Id.*
148.   *See supra* note 146 and accompanying text.
149.   *Holder*, 129 S.Ct. 2504, 2508.
150.   *Id.*
151.   *See Id.* at 2509–13 (noting the quantifiable improvements in Black voter registration and participation and providing a pessimistic rationale for the VRA's continued existence in the future).

152.   *Revelation* 21:1-6.
153.   *See,* e.g., Press Release, United States Environmental Protection Agency, Obama Administration Advances Efforts to Protect Health of U.S. Communities Overburdened by Pollution (Aug. 4, 2011), available at: http://yosemite.epa.gov/opa/admpress.nsf/bd4379a92ceceeac8525 735900400c27/28420a5ae8467cf5852578e200635712!OpenDocument (last visited March 11, 2014)(stating that "[a]ll too often, low-income, minority and Native Americans live in the shadows of our society's worst pollution, facing disproportionate health impacts and greater obstacles to economic growth.... [E]nvironmental justice [is one] ... of my top priorities for the work of the EPA, and we're glad to have [the] President['s] ... leadership....") (internal citations omitted); *see also* Juliet Eilperin, *Environmental Justice Issues Take Center Stage,* WASH. POST (Nov. 21, 2010, 8:23 PM)("Obama administration officials are looking at hazardous waste storage, toxic air emissions and an array of other contaminants to try to determine whether low-income and minority communities are disproportionately exposed to them."). Further, under the leadership of Administrator Lisa Jackson, the EPA has also released a comprehensive environmental justice strategy plan. *See generally, Plan EJ 2014,* UNITED STATES ENVIRONMENTAL PROTECTION AGENCY (September 2011), available at: http://www.epa.gov/environmentaljustice/resources/policy/plan-ej-2014/plan-ej-2011-09.pdf (last visited March 11, 2014).
154.   *See,* e.g., Robert R. Kuehn, *Denying Access to Legal Representation: The Attack on the Tulane Environmental Law Clinic,* 4 WASH. U. J.L. & POL'Y 33 (2000) (discussing the well-publicized community friction between former Louisiana Governor Murphy J. "Mike" Foster, the then-leadership of the Tulane Environmental Law Clinic, and the Louisiana Supreme Court's modification of standards for student attorneys/clinicians to assist clients after the clinic's success in pursuing environmental discrimination claims against the Shintech Corporation).
155.   As an example of the Obama Administration's ecological focus, part of the American Recovery and Reinvestment Act of 2009, Pub. L. 111-5, 123 Stat. 115, 516 (also referred to as The Stimulus or ARRA), allocated $78.6 billion for developing environmentally friendly jobs to help jumpstart the

United States' then-lagging economy. *See generally* Tracey de Morsella, *The Stimulus Bill Includes Numerous Green Initiatives—Find Out Exactly What They Are*, THE GREEN ECONOMY POST (2009), http://greeneconomypost.com/stimulus-bill-green-initiatives-533.htm (last visited March 11, 2014); *see also* Jonathan C. Augustine, *A National Model for Disaster Recovery: Growing Green Jobs in the Age of Energy Efficiency*, 37 T. MARSHALL L. REV. 179 (2012).

156.   John C. Dernbach, *Creating the Law of Environmentally Sustainable Economic Development*, 28 PACE ENVTL. L. REV. 614, 615 (2011) (internal citations omitted).

157.   Laura Kerns, *The Context of Eco-theology*, in THE BLACKWELL COMPANION TO MODERN THEOLOGY 466, 467-68 (Gareth Jones ed., 2004) (arguing that religious ecology regards God's *Genesis* 1:28 gift of "dominion" to humankind as implying a stewardship to care for creation).

158.   *See, e.g.,* CLIFFORD RECHTSCHAFFEN, EILEEN GAUNA & CATHERINE A. O'NEILL, ENVIRONMENTAL JUSTICE: LAW, POLICY & REGULATION 3-4 (2009); Alice Kaswan, *Environmental Justice: Bridging the Gap Between Environmental Laws and "Justice"*, 47 AM. U. L. REV. 221, 225-28 (1997). For a more-detailed analysis of the environmental justice movement, *see generally*, ROBERT D. BULLARD, UNEQUAL PROTECTION: ENVIRONMENTAL JUSTICE AND COMMUNITIES OF COLOR (1994).

159.   The term eschatology (last things from the Greek word *eschatos* (last) and *logos* (word) is commonly used in the theological academy to denote a belief in the *Parousia* (second coming of Jesus Christ) and the anticipated end of the world. MARIAN L. SOARDS, THE APOSTLE PAUL: AN INTRODUCTION TO HIS WRITINGS AND TEACHINGS 199 (1987) (defining *Parousia* as the second coming of Jesus, the foretold messiah, and explaining its messianic influence on the Apostle Paul's theology); JAIME CLARK-SOLES, ENGAGING THE WORD: THE NEW TESTAMENT AND THE CHRISTIAN BELIEVER 78 (2010) (discussing eschatology in the authentic Pauline epistles); *see also* JAMES H. CONE, A BLACK THEOLOGY OF LIBERATION: TWENTIETH ANNIVERSARY EDITION 135 (1990) (defining eschatology as a study of the future; that which is called the "last things."). Indeed, a theology of eschatology is prevalent in the New Testament. *See, e.g.,* 1 *Corinthians* 7:8-9, (writing to the church at Corinth, the Apostle Paul encouraged women not to marry and have children because

there was a fundamental belief that there simply was not enough time in that Jesus' second coming was imminent).

160. *See, e.g.,* Barbara R. Rossing, *For the Healing of the World: Reading Revelation Ecologically, in* FROM EVERY PEOPLE AND NATION: THE BOOK OF REVELATION IN INTERCULTURAL PERSPECTIVE (David Rhoads ed., 2005), at 165 (providing an exegetical commentary on *Revelation* and other biblical texts from an ecological perspective); *see also* PAUL SANTMIRE, THE TRAVAIL OF NATURE: THE AMBIGUOUS ECOLOGICAL PROMISE OF CHRISTIAN THEOLOGY 200 (1985) (discussing the New Testament as being shaped by ecological motif, albeit eschatologically construed).

161. As an example, theologians Owen Thomas and Ellen Wondra provide a historical basis of eschatology in Judeo-Christian philosophy, writing that: "...during the early Christian centuries, eschatological teaching amounted largely to the exposition of the biblical themes of the *parousia*, the general resurrection, the last judgment, heaven, and hell. A unique feature of early eschatological teaching was the widespread affirmation of millennialism, the idea that, at the *parousia*, Christ will reign on earth with the saints for a thousand years before the final fulfillment." OWEN C. THOMAS & ELLEN K. WONDRA, INTRODUCTION TO THEOLOGY 245 (3d ed. 2002) (citing *Revelation* 20:4f).

162. *See generally* Charlton C. Copeland, *God-Talk in the Age of Obama: Theology and Religious Political Engagement*, 86 DENV. U. L. REV. 663, 663 n.6 (2009) (discussing the controversy of then-candidate Obama's membership in Trinity United Church of Christ and long-term association with its former pastor, the Rev. Dr. Jeremiah A. Wright).

163. For specific imagery of a "rapture in reverse," whereby God comes down to earth to live, *see, e.g., Revelation* 21:10 ("And in the spirit he carried me away to a great, high mountain and showed me the holy city Jerusalem *coming down out of heaven from God.*") (emphasis added); *see also Revelation* 21:2 ("And I saw the holy city, the new Jerusalem, coming down out of the heaven from God . . . .). Anecdotally, although *Revelation* is arguably the least favorite book in the Bible for many regular worshipers and biblical readers, scholars like Barbara Rossing, a professor of the New Testament at the Lutheran School of Theology at Chicago, advocate reading

Revelation—especially its last two chapters—as revealing a message of hope and love from God as believers prepare for the world's apocalyptic end. *See generally* Barbara R. Rossing, *Introduction to the Revelation Study,* http://www.youtube.com/watch?v=n_03axPvnMQ (last visited March 11, 2014).

164. Brian K. Blount, *Revelation, in* TRUE TO OUR NATIVE LAND: AN AFRICAN AMERICAN NEW TESTAMENT COMMENTARY 523 (Brian K. Blount ed., 2007).

165. *Id.,* at 523; *see also* PAUL J. ACHTEMEIER, JOEL B. GREEN & MARIANNE MEYE THOMPSON, INTRODUCING THE NEW TESTAMENT: ITS LITERATURE AND THEOLOGY 564 (2001) (*"Revelation* does not order these logically and neatly into an end-time scenario, but recasts apocalyptic eschatology in light of John's Christian theology and immediate pastoral concerns.").

166. *Id.* Furthermore, in exploring *Revelation's* salvific beauty, Professor Blount writes that "[w]ith even death destroyed, eternal life parades into a scene so glorious that John can only describe it as a cosmic wedding in a brilliant new city whose name is Jerusalem, but whose heritage is Eden." *Id.* at 525. Indeed, this eternal relationship with God describes salvation.

167. David Rhoads, *Introduction, in* FROM EVERY PEOPLE AND NATION: THE BOOK OF REVELATION IN INTERCULTURAL PERSPECTIVE 1 (David Rhoads ed., 2005) (emphasis added) (providing the introduction to a cultural anthology of African, feminist, Hispanic, womanist, immigrant, Brazilian, African-American, and ecological interpretations of *Revelation*). The concept of "withdrawal" builds upon Jewish tradition as it is reminiscent of God withdrawing the Hebrew slaves from Egypt under Moses' leadership. *See Exodus* 13-14.

168. The "eternal spring" is expressly described in *Revelation* 22:1. For an excellent cultural exegesis of *Revelation* 21-22 as providing hope to marginalized Blacks, *see generally* Blount, *supra* note 164, at 553-54 (drawing a parallel between John's transformative imagery in *Revelation* to Dr. King's transformative imagery in the famous August 1963 "I Have A Dream" speech); BRIAN K. BLOUNT, CAN I GET A WITNESS? READING *REVELATION* THROUGH AN AFRICAN AMERICAN LENS (2005); *see also* Brian K. Blount, *The Witness of Active Resistance: The Ethics of* Revelation *in African American*

169

Jonathan C. Augustine

Perspective, in FROM EVERY PEOPLE AND NATION: THE BOOK OF
REVELATION IN INTERCULTURAL PERSPECTIVE 28 (David Rhoads
ed., 2005).
    169.   *See generally* Barbara Rossing, *River of Life in
God's New Jerusalem: An Ecological Vision for Earth's Future, in*
CHRISTIANITY AND ECOLOGY 206 (Dieter T. Hessel & Rosemary
Ranford Ruether eds., 1999).
    170.   Blount, *supra* note 21, at 524-25; *see also*
Rossing, *supra* note 11, at 167. For other images of a "new" or
heavenly Jerusalem, *see, e.g., Tobit* 13:16-17, 14:5-7
(apocryphal/deuterocanonical scriptures); *see also Galatians*
4:21-31.
    171.   *See, e.g.,* 1 *Thessalonians* 4:16-17 (describing
how the Lord will descend from heaven and humans will be
caught up in the clouds to meet him).
    172.   *Revelation* 21:2-3.
    173.   *Id.*
    174.   *Id.*
    175.   *Id.*
    176.   *Revelation* 21:10 (emphasis added).
    177.   *Revelation* 21:2-3.
    178.   Blount, *supra* note 164, at 523.
    179.   Rossing, *supra* note 160, at 172.
    180.   *Id.*
    181.   *Id.; see also Revelation* 8:13, 12:12.
    182.   Rossing, *supra* note 160, at 172.
    183.   *Id.*
    184.   *See id.* at 173.
    185.   *Revelation* 11:18 (explaining the wrath of God's
judgment and how those that destroy the Earth will themselves
be destroyed).
    186.   Rossing, *supra* note 160, at 174.
    187.   *See generally,* ELISABETH SCHUSSLER FIORENZA,
REVELATION: VISION OF A JUST WORLD (1998).
    188.   *See generally, Exodus* 15:1-19 (detailing the Song
of Moses sung by the Israelites in praising God for delivering
them from bondage in Egypt and destroying their oppressors);
see also Rossing, *supra* note 160, at 175 (arguing that John's
visions of plagues and destruction in *Revelation* are directly
based on the plagues detailed in *Exodus* and the destruction of
the Egyptians who oppressed the Israelites).

189. *See Exodus* 15:1-4; *see also Revelation* 18:4 ("Then I heard another voice from heaven saying, 'Come out of her, my people, so that you do not take part in her sins, and so that you do not share in her plagues' . . . .").

190. *See generally Revelation* 16 (providing a narrative account of the consequences for oppressors who commit injustices, resulting from the instruction given to seven angels to pour out the wrath of God). Indeed, God's wrath in *Revelation* 16 is almost identical to certain Old Testament texts. *See, e.g., Exodus* 7:17-21; *see also Isaiah* 49:26.

191. Rossing, *supra* note 160, at 177 (internal citations omitted).

192. *Id.* at 177 (internal citations omitted).

193. Kaswan, *supra* note 158, at 226.

194. *Id.*

195. *Id.*

196. *Id.*

197. *See generally* ROBERT D. BULLARD, PAUL MOHAI, ROBIN SAHA & BEVERLY WRIGHT, TOXIC WASTE AND RACE AT TWENTY: 1987-2007 (March 2007), available at: http://www.ucc.org/assets/pdfs/toxic20.pdf (last visited March 11, 2014).

198. Executive Order 12,898 was entitled "Federal Actions to Address Environmental Justice in Minority Populations and Low-Income Populations." *See* Exec. Order No. 12,898, 3 C.F.R. § 859 (1995).

199. *Id.* at 245 (internal citations omitted).

200. Kaswan, *supra* note 158, at 246 (citing *President's Memorandum on Environmental Justice*, 30 WKLY. COMPILATION PRESIDENTIAL DOC. 279, 280 (Feb. 11, 1994)).

201. *See, e.g.,* Carlton Waterhouse, *Abandon All Hope Ye That Enter? Equal Protection, Title VI, and the Divine Comedy of Environmental Justice*, 20 FORDHAM ENVTL. L. REV. 51, 105-11 (2009) (discussing failed 2007 legislation filed in the House and Senate, by then-Rep. Hilda Solis and Senator Richard Durbin, and emphasizing the importance of President Clinton's Executive Order 12,898 being codified into law).

202. Andrea Simpson, *Who Hears Their Cry?: African American Women and the Fight for Environmental Justice in Memphis, Tennessee, in* THE ENVIRONMENTAL JUSTICE READER:

POLITICS, POETICS & PEDAGOGY 82, 83 (Joni Adamson, Mei
Evans & Rachel Stein eds., 2002).
    203. Carlton Waterhouse, *Dr. King's Speech:
Surveying the Landscape of Law and Justice in the Speeches,
Sermons, and Writings of Dr. Martin Luther King, Jr.*, 30 LAW &
INEQ. 91, 99 (2012).
    204. Definitions of "environmental justice" may vary.
According to recent scholarship, however, "[e]nvironmental
justice is the desire and the demand that poor and oppressed
people in the United States and around the world be provided
with the protection, consideration, and decision-making
authority provided to their wealthier or whiter counterparts
locally and globally." Carlton Waterhouse, *Failed Plans and
Planned Failures: The Lower Ninth Ward, Hurricane Katrina,
and the Continuing Story of Environmental Injustice*, in
HURRICANE KATRINA: AMERICA'S UNNATURAL DISASTER 157
(Jeremy I. Levitt & Matthew C. Whitaker eds., 2009). Moreover,
Professor Waterhouse also draws a direct link from the
Movement's acts of civil disobedience in the 1960s to the origins
of environmental justice in Warren County, North Carolina. *Id.*;
see also Carlton Waterhouse, *Abandon All Hope Ye That Enter?
Equal Protection, Title VI, and the Divine Comedy of
Environmental Justice*, 20 FORDHAM ENVTL. L. REV. 51, 57–59
(2009) (describing the environmental justice movement as
originating with direct action tactics and civil rights "campaigns"
designed to address the issue of environmental racism). Further,
in also attempting to provide a definition to clarify the inherent
ambiguity of the term environmental justice, Bob Kuehn, a
nationally reputed environmental law professor, writes that:
"Environmental justice" means many things to many people. To
local communities feeling overburdened by environmental
hazards and left out of the decision making process, it captures
their sense of the unfairness of the development,
implementation, and enforcement of environmental laws and
policies. To regulated entities facing allegations that they have
created or contributed to injustices, environmental justice is an
amorphous term that wrongly suggests racial-based or class-
based animus or, at the very least, indifference to the public
health and welfare of distressed communities.... To
governmental officials often the target of environmental justice

activists' ire, the term may imply that they are executing their responsibilities in a biased or callous manner.
Robert R. Kuehn, *A Taxonomy of Environmental Justice*, 30 ENVTL. L. REP. 10681, 10681 (2000).
    205.   Some would argue that the election of President John F. Kennedy, an Irish Catholic at a time when Catholicism was not widely accepted in the U.S., and the U.S.'s first Irish Catholic president, was the socio-religious precedent for the election of Barack Obama in the Nation's history.
    206.   *See, e.g., Obama Administration Advances Efforts to Protect Health of U.S. Communities Overburdened by Pollution / Federal Agencies Sign Environmental Justice Memorandum of Understanding*, U.S. ENVTL. PROT. AGENCY (Aug. 4, 2011), available at: http://yosemite.epa.gov/opa/admpress.nsf/bd4379a92ceceeac8525 735900400c27/28420a5ae8467cf5852578e200635712!OpenDocum ent (last visited March 11, 2014)("All too often, low-income, minority and Native Americans live in the shadows of our society's worst pollution, facing disproportionate health impacts and greater obstacles to economic growth . . . . [E]nvironmental justice [is one] . . . of my top priorities for the work of the EPA, and we're glad to have [the] President['s] . . . leadership . . . ." (internal citations omitted)); *see also* Juliet Eilperin, *Environmental Justice Issues Take Center Stage*, WASH. POST (Nov. 10, 2010), available at: http://www.washingtonpost.com/wp-dyn/content/article/2010/11/21/AR2010112103782.html (last visited March 11, 2014)("Obama administration officials are looking at hazardous waste storage, toxic air emissions and an array of other contaminants to try to determine whether low-income and minority communities are disproportionately exposed to them.").
Further, under the leadership of Administrator Lisa Jackson, the EPA has also released a comprehensive environmental justice strategy plan. *See generally* U.S. ENVTL. PROT. AGENCY, PLAN EJ 2014 (2011), available at: http://www.epa.gov/environmentaljustice/resources/policy/plan-ej-2014/plan-ej-2011-09.pdf (last visited March 11, 2014).
    207.   *Remarks by the President in State of Union Address*, THE WHITE HOUSE: OFFICE OF THE PRESS SECRETARY (Jan. 25, 2011), available at: http://www.whitehouse.gov/the-

press-office/2011/01/25/remarks-president-state-union-address (last visited March 11, 2014).

208. American Recovery and Reinvestment Act of 2009 ("ARRA") (a.k.a "The Stimulus"), Pub. L. No. 111-5, 123 Stat. 115 (2009). The Stimulus was passed by Congress on February 13, 2009 and signed into law by President Obama four days later, on February 17th.

209. *See generally* Jonathan C. Augustine & Hon. Ulysses Gene Thibodeaux, *Forty Years Later: Chronicling the Voting Rights Act of 1965 and its Impact on Louisiana's Judiciary*, 66 LA. L. REV. 453, 478–80 (2006) (discussing some of the South's racial problems in voting such that African-Americans were required to seek governmental intervention by making Equal Protection Clause challenges); *see also* Jonathan C. Augustine, *Rethinking* Shaw v. Reno*, the Supreme Court's Benign Race-Related Jurisprudence and Louisiana's Recent Reapportionment: The Argument for Intermediate Scrutiny in Racial Gerrymandering According to the Voting Rights Act*, 29 S.U. L. REV. 151 (2002) (discussing the problem of race in Louisiana, such that the Voting Rights Act remains a necessity to ensure fair and equitable elections).

210. Part of the environmental justice movement addresses the issue of "distributive justice," disproportionately siting locally undesirable land uses, or "LULUs," in poor and minority communities. *See generally* Shelia Foster, *Justice from the Ground Up: Distributive Inequalities, Grassroots Resistance, and the Transformative Politics of the Environmental Justice Movement*, 86 CALIF. L. REV. 775, 788–98 (1998) (discussing distributive justice and process theories of justice); *see also* Vicki Been, *Locally Undesirable Land Uses in Minority Neighborhoods: Disproportionate Siting or Market Dynamics?*, 103 YALE L.J. 1383, 1384 & n.2 (1994) (citing studies analyzing the relationship between the socioeconomic characteristics of neighborhoods and the number of LULUs within them). This Article does not attempt to comprehensively address the nuances of distributive justice. For an excellent analysis of distributive justice as part of the environmental justice movement, see Alice Kaswan, *Distributive Justice and the Environment*, 81 N.C. L. REV. 1031 (2003). This Article does show, however, that through environmental advancement, the Deep South is leading a new environmental justice movement.

211. Definitions of "green" may vary, as no commonly accepted definition has emerged. For discussion purposes, however, "green jobs" are defined as those that have a primary job function wherein more than 50 percent of the employee's time is spent in one or more of seven green activity categories: Renewable Energy; Energy Efficiency; Greenhouse Gas Reduction; Pollution Reduction and Clean-up; Recycling and Waste Reduction; Sustainable Agriculture, Natural Resource Conservation, and Costal Restoration; and Education, Compliance, Public Awareness and Training Supporting Other Categories. LA. WORKFORCE COMM'N, THE GREENING OF LOUISIANA'S ECONOMY: SUMMARY OF SURVEY RESULTS 1 (2011), [hereinafter SUMMARY RESULTS], available at: http://lwc.laworks.net/sites/LMI/GreenJobs/Reports/Louisiana_S urvey_Results.pdf#Intro (last visited March 11, 2014).

212. *La. Awarded $10 Million Federal Grant for Oil Spill-Related Re-employment Services Additional $3.4 Million in Grants Awarded for Other Re-employment Needs*, LA. WORKFORCE COMM'N (June 30, 2010), http://www.laworks.net/PublicRelations/PR_PressReleaseDetails .asp?SeqNo=1044&Year=2010&Month=6 (last visited March 11, 2014); LA. WORKFORCE COMM'N, WORKFORCE INVESTMENT ACT PROGRAM YEAR 2010: ANNUAL REPORT 13 (2011), http://www.laworks.net/Downloads/WFD/WIAAnnualReport_201 0.pdf (last visited March 11, 2014). Further, in issuing the $10 million NEG funds to the LWC, USDOL's program participant eligibility requirements included individuals that were dislocated, either permanently or temporarily, or unable to work because of the disaster. *Id.*

213. Waterhouse, *Dr. King's Speech, supra* note 203, at 101–02 (internal citations omitted).

214. For a comprehensive discussion of the social gospel compelling those active in ministry to also be active in ensuring societal justice, see WALTER RAUSCHENBUSCH, A THEOLOGY FOR THE SOCIAL GOSPEL (1918); A RAUSCHENBUSCH READER: THE KINGDOM OF GOD AND THE SOCIAL GOSPEL (Benson Y. Landis ed., 1957). As a result of his seminary studies, King was undoubtedly influenced by the theology of Walter Rauschenbusch, a Baptist minister and professor of church history, who "believed that the American democracy undergirded by Christian morality represented a new era of social progress."

Janet Forsythe Fishburn, *Walter Rauschenbusch and "The Woman Movement"*: *A Gender Analysis, in* GENDER AND THE SOCIAL GOSPEL (Wendy J. Deichmann Edwards & Carolyn De Swarte Gifford eds., 2003), at 71. Further, King also credited his studies of Rauschenbusch and Gandhi's ethics of nonviolence as a basis for his social views. *See* Michael Dwayne Blackwell, *In the Legacy of Martin Luther King Jr.: the Social Gospel of Faye Wattleton and Marian Wright Edelman, in* GENDER AND THE SOCIAL GOSPEL (Wendy J. Deichmann Edwards & Carolyn De Swarte Gifford eds., 2003), at 217. Indeed, King's social perspective as a pastor must have been influenced by Judeo-Christian thought. As other scholarship provides, the "formative religious traditions of the Western world—Judaism and Christianity—have for millennia embraced the conviction that their religious duty entailed active intervention in the 'body politic.' As a result, . . . churches and synagogues can no more be silent on public issues than human beings can refrain from breathing." Daniel O. Conkle, *Secular Fundamentalism, Religious Fundamentalism, and the Search for Truth in Contemporary America, in* LAW & RELIGION: A CRITICAL ANTHOLOGY 326 (Stephen M. Feldman ed., 2000) (footnote and internal quotations omitted).

    215. *See, e.g.,* DAVID J. GARROW, BEARING THE CROSS: MARTIN LUTHER KING, JR. AND THE SOUTHERN CHRISTIAN LEADERSHIP CONFERENCE (1986); A TESTAMENT OF HOPE, *supra* note 3; MARTIN LUTHER KING, JR., WHERE DO WE GO FROM HERE: CHAOS OR COMMUNITY (1968); THE AUTOBIOGRAPHY OF MARTIN LUTHER KING, JR. (Clayborne Carson ed., 1998).

    216. Waterhouse, *Dr. King's Speech, supra* note 203, at 92–93 (internal citations omitted).

    217. The Voting Rights Act of 1965, Pub. L. No. 89-110, 79 Stat. 437 (1965) (codified as 42 U.S.C. § 1973 *et seq.* (2006)), was signed into law by President Lyndon Johnson on August 6, 1965. See DAVID J. GARROW, PROTEST AT SELMA: MARTIN LUTHER KING, JR. AND THE VOTING RIGHTS ACT OF 1965 xi (1979).

    218. Theologians define the Greek word agape as a love or an allegiance shared by members of a group. *See, e.g.,* BRUCE J. MALINA & JOHN J. PILCH, SOCIAL SCIENCE COMMENTARY ON THE LETTERS OF PAUL 116–18 (2006); Yxta Maya Murray, *A Jurisprudence of Nonviolence*, 9 CONN. PUB.

INT. L.J. 65, 73–74 (2009) (describing King's philosophy of love as agape).

219. PETER J. PARIS, BLACK RELIGIOUS LEADERS: CONFLICT IN UNITY 108–09 (1991); *see also* HOWARD THURMAN, WITH HEAD AND HEART: THE AUTOBIOGRAPHY OF HOWARD THURMAN 113–14 (1979) (discussing his allegiance to Christianity because of its core principles); HOWARD THURMAN, JESUS AND THE DISINHERITED 11–35 (1949) (explaining the religion of Jesus Christ as one who was an advocate for the marginalized in society).

220. *Id.*, at 118.

221. *See* Colin Crawford, *Strategies for Environmental Justice: Rethinking CERCLA Medical Monitoring Lawsuits*, 74 B.U. L. REV. 267, 268–69 (1994) (discussing the 1982 North Carolina arrests of noted civil rights activists including United Church of Christ Executive Director Dr. Benjamin Chavis, Jr., Congressman Fauntrory, and Dr. Joseph Lowery, president of the Southern Christian Leadership Conference, because of their protests of North Carolina's ultimately successful effort to place a dump for highly toxic polychlorinated biphenyls in mainly Black community of Warren County); William C. Scott, *Environmental Justice: A New Era of Community Empowerment, Political Activism, and Civil Rights Litigation*, 7 ENVTL. CLAIMS J. 5, 11 (1994) (noting that grassroots environmental justice groups applied the same techniques as civil rights activists); Waterhouse, *Environmental Injustice, supra* note 203, at 157 (arguing that under the leadership of then-Congressmen Walter E. Fauntrory, Warren County, North Carolina's residents used "campaigns" made popular during the Movement); *see also* Robert D. Bullard & Beverly H. Wright, *The Quest for Environmental Equity: Mobilizing the African American Community for Social Changes, in* AMERICAN ENVIRONMENTALISM (Riley E. Dunlap & Angela G. Mertig eds., 1992), at 39 (arguing the environmental justice movement's origins were inspired by the civil rights and antiwar movements of the 1960s).

222. LUKE COLE & SHEILA FOSTER, FROM THE GROUND UP: ENVIRONMENTAL RACISM AND THE RISE OF THE ENVIRONMENTAL JUSTICE MOVEMENT 19–28 (2001). Indeed, it was not until the 1990s that more traditional academicians began to see the value in environmental justice as a basis of

sound scholarship. *See, e.g.*, Richard J. Lazarus, *Pursuing "Environmental Justice": The Distributional Effects of Environmental Protection*, 87 NW. U. L. REV. 787, 790 (1993).

223. *See*, e.g., Benjamin F. Chavis, Jr., *Foreword* to CONFRONTING ENVIRONMENTAL RACISM: VOICES FROM THE GRASSROOTS 3 (Robert D. Bullard ed., 1993).

224. Kaswan, *Environmental Justice, supra* note 210, at 226. There was also a follow-up to the 1987 United Church of Christ Report, published twenty-years after its initial findings were made public. *See generally* ROBERT D. BULLARD ET AL., UNITED CHURCH OF CHRIST: JUSTICE & WITNESS MINISTRIES, TOXIC WASTE AND RACE AT TWENTY: 1987–2007 (2007), available at: http://www.ucc.org/assets/pdfs/toxic20.pdf (last visited March 11, 2014).

225. Kaswan, *Environmental Justice, supra* note 210, at 226.

226. RECHTSCHAFFEN ET AL., *supra* note 158, at 24.

227. *Id.* at 24–25. The Principles of Environmental Justice were adopted October 24, 1991 in Washington, D.C. *Id.*

228. *See* Kaswan, *Environmental Justice, supra* note 210, at 244–45. Executive Order 12,898 was entitled "Federal Actions To Address Environmental Justice in Minority Populations and Low-Income Populations." *See generally* Exec. Order No. 12,898, 3 C.F.R. § 859 (1995).

229. *Id.*

230. *Id.* at 245 (internal citations omitted).

231. ERICA WILLIAMS ET AL., INST. FOR WOMEN'S POLICY RESEARCH, THE WOMEN OF NEW ORLEANS AND THE GULF COAST: MULTIPLE DISADVANTAGES AND KEY ASSETS FOR RECOVERY 1 (2006), available at: http://www.iwpr.org/publications/pubs/the-women-of-new-orleans-and-the-gulf-coast-multiple-disadvantages-and-key-assets-for-recovery-part-ii.-gender-race-and-class-in-the-labor-market/at_download/file (last visited March 11, 2014).

232. SELECT BIPARTISAN COMM. TO INVESTIGATE THE PREPARATION FOR & RESPONSE TO HURRICANE KATRINA, 109TH CONG., A FAILURE OF INITIATIVE, at 111 (2006).

233. William P. Quigley, *What Katrina Revealed*, 2 HARV. L. & POL'Y REV. 361, 362 (2008) [hereinafter Quigley, *What Katrina Revealed*].

THE KEYS ARE BEING PASSED

234. For an excellent exegetical review of environmentalism in the Book of Revelation, *see* Barbara R. Rossing, *For the Healing of the World: Reading Revelation Ecologically, in* FROM EVERY PEOPLE AND NATION: THE BOOK OF REVELATION IN INTERCULTURAL PERSPECTIVE 165 (David Rhoads, ed. 2005) [hereinafter Rossing, *Reading Revelation Ecologically*]; PAUL SANTMIRE, THE TRAVAIL OF NATURE: THE AMBIGUOUS ECOLOGICAL PROMISE OF CHRISTIAN THEOLOGY 200 (1985) (discussing the New Testament as being shaped by ecological motif, albeit eschatological construed); Presbyterian Women, *Introduction to the Revelation Study*, http://www.youtube.com/watch?v=n_03axPvnMQ (last visited March 11, 2014).

235. The term eschatology (last things from the Greek word *eschatos* "last" and *logos* "word") is commonly used in the theological academy to denote a belief in the *Parousia* (second coming of Jesus Christ) and the anticipated end of the world. *See* MARIAN L. SOARDS, THE APOSTLE PAUL: AN INTRODUCTION TO HIS WRITINGS AND TEACHINGS 199–200 (1987) (defining *parousia* as the second coming of Jesus, the foretold messiah, and explaining its messianic influence on the Apostle Paul's theology); JAIME CLARK-SOLES, ENGAGING THE WORD: THE NEW TESTAMENT AND THE CHRISTIAN BELIEVER 78–79 (2010) (same); JAMES H. CONE, A BLACK THEOLOGY OF LIBERATION: TWENTIETH ANNIVERSARY EDITION 135 (1990) (defining eschatology as a study of the future; that which is called the "last things").

236. *See generally* Barbara Rossing, *River of Life in God's New Jerusalem: An Ecological Vision for Earth's Future, in* CHRISTIANITY AND ECOLOGY 206 (Dieter T. Hessel & Rosemary Ranford Ruether eds., 1999).

237. BRIAN K. BLOUNT, *Revelation, in* TRUE TO OUR NATIVE LAND: AN AFRICAN AMERICAN NEW TESTAMENT COMMENTARY 523, 524–25 (Brian K. Blount ed., 2007); *see also* Rossing, *Reading Revelation Ecologically, supra* note 158, at 167. For other images of a "new" or heavenly Jerusalem, see *Tobit* 13:16–17, 14:5–7 (apocryphal/deuterocanonical scriptures); *see also Galatians* 4:21–31.

238. From a theological perspective, King might indeed support this position, especially in light of *Revelation's* contrast between imperial (corporate) domination and an organizing community rejecting such imperialism. *See*

RECHTSCHAFFEN ET AL., *supra* note 158, at 25 (fourteenth Principle of Environmental Justice manifesting a rejection of corporate imperialism and destruction of the Earth).

239.	See *Revelation* 21: 2–3.

240.	*Id.*

241.	Earth Day is officially recognized as April 22nd of each year.

242.	*See* Laura Kerns, *The Context of Eco-theology, in* THE BLACKWELL COMPANION TO MODERN THEOLOGY 466, 467–68 (Gareth Jones ed., 2004) (arguing that religious ecology regards God's *Genesis* 1:28 gift of "dominion" to humankind as implying a stewardship to care for creation).

243.	James Foreman, Jr., *The Secret History of School Choice: How Progressives Got There First*, 93 GEO. L.J. 1287, 1296 (2005) (emphasis added); *see also* SEE FOREVER FOUND. & MAYA ANGELOU CHARTER SCH., http://seeforever.org/ (last visited March 11, 2014).

244.	*Id.* at 331–32. For an argument of *Grutter* as a reaffirmation of *Brown*, see Harry T. Edwards, *The Journey from Brown v. Board of Education to Grutter v. Bollinger: From Racial Assimilation to Diversity*, 102 MICH. L. REV. 944, 946 (2004).

245.	Elementary and Secondary Education Act of 1965, Pub. L. No. 89-10, 79 Stat. 27–58 (codified as amended in scattered sections of 20 U.S.C.). ESEA's currently enforced version is NCLB. President Obama's proposed NCLB amendments are publically available. *See generally* U.S. DEP'T OF EDUC., A BLUEPRINT FOR REFORM: THE REAUTHORIZATION OF THE ELEMENTARY AND SECONDARY EDUCATION ACT (2010), available	at: http://www2.ed.gov/policy/elsec/leg/blueprint/blueprint.pdf (last visited March 11, 2014). They outline four areas for NCLB reform, aligned with RTT: (1) improving teacher and principal effectiveness; (2) providing adequate information and data to families and educators; (3) implementing standards and assessments to ensure all graduates are college and career ready; and (4) improving student performance in the lowest performing schools.

246.	No Child Left Behind Act of 2001, Pub. L. No. 107-110, 115 Stat. 1425 (codified at 20 U.S.C. §§ 6301–7941 (2006)). Congress passed NCLB as a bipartisan means of improving the quality of public education. On December 13, 2001, the House of Representatives passed the bill with 381 votes. *See Final Vote Results for Roll Call 497*, U.S. HOUSE OF REPRESENTATIVES (Dec. 13, 2001). Similarly, it passed the Senate with 87 votes. *See Roll Call Vote on H.R. 1 (No Child Left Behind Act of 2001)*, U.S. SENATE (Dec. 18, 2001).

247. In fairness to both administrations, the Department of Education is still relatively new, having been established at the cabinet level in 1980. U.S. DEP'T OF EDUC., http://www2.ed.gov/about/ overview/fed/role.html?src=ln (last visited March 11, 2014). Considering the Department's brief history, one can argue President Bush made great strides with NCLB's bipartisan passage. *See generally* George W. Bush, Remarks on Implementation of the No Child Left Behind Act of 2001 (Sept. 4, 2002), available at: http://www.presidency.ucsb.edu/ws/index.php?pid=73078#axzz1q vklzovq (last visited March 11, 2014). For an historical analysis of education in the United States, see Sandy Kress et al., *When Performance Matters: The Past Present, and Future of Consequential Accountability in Public Education*, 48 HARV. J. LEGIS. 185, 187–94 (2011); *see also* Jonathan C. Augustine & Craig M. Freeman, *Grading the Graders and Reforming the Reform: The State of Public Education Ten Years After No Child Left Behind*, 57 LOY. L. REV. 237, 247–50 (2011).

248. Notwithstanding NCLB's unprecedented reform measures, the Obama Administration announced NCLB waivers, along with its own original education reform initiative, called "Race to the Top." Speaking about the initiative, President Obama said: "When a child walks into a classroom, it should be a place of high expectations and high performance. But too many schools don't meet this test. That's why instead of just pouring money into a system that's not working, we launched a competition called Race to the Top. To all 50 states, we said, 'If you show us the most innovative plans to improve teacher quality and student achievement, we'll show you the money.' Race to the Top is the most meaningful reform of our public schools in a generation. For less than 1 percent of what we spend on education each year, it has led over 40 states to raise their standards for teaching and learning. And these standards were developed, by the way, not by Washington, but by

Republican and Democratic governors throughout the country. And Race to the Top should be the approach we follow this year as we replace No Child Left Behind with a law that's more flexible and focused on what's best for our kids." Barack Obama, Address Before a Joint Session of the Congress on the State of the Union (Jan. 25, 2011), available at: http://www.presidency.ucsb.edu/ws/index.php?pid=88928 (last visited March 11, 2014).
See also Helene Cooper, *Obama Urges Education Law Overhaul*, N.Y. TIMES, Mar. 14, 2011, at A24, available at: http://www.nytimes.com/2011/03/15/us/politics/15obama.html?_r =2&ref=nochildleftbehindact. (last visited March 11, 2014).
Regardless of their differences, Presidents Bush and Obama are clearly united in their desire to systemically improve education.

249.   *See generally* Derrick A. Bell, Jr., Comment, Brown v. Board *and the Interest-Convergence Dilemma*, 93 HARV. L. REV. 518 (1980).

250.   *Id.* at 524-25.

251.   For an analysis and application of Professor Bell's interest convergence theory from a White perspective, see generally Robert A. Garda, Jr., *The White Interest in School Integration*, 63 FLA. L. REV. 599 (2011) (arguing diversity in education benefits whites and society as a whole). "The interest convergence theory conveys an ugly truth—whites (or any empowered group) will not help minorities (or any disempowered group) unless it is in their best interest to do so." *Id.* at 603.

252.   *Our Mission and Beliefs*, BAEO, http://baeo.org/mission.html (last visited March 11, 2014).

253.   *See generally*, Sonja Ralston Elder, *Adding Autonomous Schools to New Orleans' Menu of School Choice*, 11 LOY. J. PUB. INT. L. 389, 389–90 (2010); *see also* Sam Dillon, *Obama Looks to Lessons from Chicago in His National Education Plan*, N.Y. TIMES, Sept. 10, 2008, at A21. , available at: http://www.nytimes.com/2008/09/10/us/politics/10educate.html?p agewanted=all&_r=0. (last visited March 11, 2014)

254.   Although widely publicized as President Obama's initiative, RTT's $4.35 billion state education reform incentives are part of Congress' American Recovery and Reinvestment Act of 2009 ("ARRA"), Pub. L. No. 111-5, 123 Stat. 115, 516 (also known as "The Stimulus"). *See generally The American Recovery and Reinvestment Act of 2009; See also* Maria Gloud, *Stimulus*

Includes $5 Billion Flexible Fund for Education, WASH. POST, Feb. 14, 2009, at A10.

255. For positive critiques noting the benefits of charter schools, see generally THE EMANCIPATORY PROMISE OF CHARTER SCHOOLS (Eric Rofes & Lisa M. Stulberg, eds. 2004) (providing essays arguing that community-controlled charter schools geared toward low income children, including children of color, offer an emancipatory potential).

256. While addressing the AFT's July 2010 national convention, commending the organization for its support of charter schools and other reform-oriented measures and criticizing teacher tenure laws, Bill Gates remarked that "[b]y partnering with school districts in key states, you bolstered the states' applications for the federal Race to the Top program. This collaboration will bring crucial new funding for schools that teach some of the nation's most underserved students." Bill Gates, Speech to the American Federation of Teachers (July 10, 2010).

257. Indeed, historically, AFT's president described how her union supports new ways to evaluate and pay teachers and establish charter schools. Randi Weingartner, *The Role of Teachers in School Improvement: Lessons from the Field*, 6 HARV. L. & POL'Y REV. 9, 23–24 (2012).

258. SCOTT S. COWEN, INST. FOR PUB. EDUC. INITIATIVES AT TULANE UNIV., PUBLIC SCHOOL PERFORMANCE IN NEW ORLEANS: A SUPPLEMENT TO THE 2008 STATE OF PUBLIC EDUCATION IN NEW ORLEANS REPORT 4 (2009) (internal citations omitted).

259. Nick Lewin, *The No Child Left Behind Act of 2001: The Triumph of School Choice over Racial Desegregation*, 12 GEO. J. ON POVERTY L. & POL'Y 95, 101 (2005).

260. John H. Jackson, *From Miracle to Movement: Mandating a National Opportunity to Learn*, in THE STATE OF BLACK AMERICA 2009: MESSAGE TO THE PRESIDENT 62 (Nat'l Urban League 2009). Moreover, government's focus on education improvement significantly benefited many blacks after 1965.

261. Damon T. Hewitt, *Reauthorize, Revise, and Remember: Refocusing the No Child Left Behind Act to Fulfill Brown's Promise*, 30 YALE L. & POL'Y REV. 169, 1169 (2011).

262. MARK G. YUDOF ET AL., EDUCATIONAL POLICY AND THE LAW 921–22 (5th ed. 2012).

263.   Craig Livermore, *Racial Complexity and the Elementary and Secondary Education Act*, 26 J. C.R. & ECON. Dev. 67, 69 (2012) (emphasis added).

264.   Michael Olneck, *Economic Consequences of the Academic Achievement Gap for African Americans*, 89 MARQUETTE L. REV. 95, 100–01 (2005) (providing a quantitative, income-based analysis to support the argument that "choice" and reduced class size lead to better incomes).

265.   *Id.*, at 101.

266.   Marian Wright Edelman, *A Call to End Adult Hypocrisy, Neglect and Abandonment of Children and America's Cradle to Prison Pipeline, in* AMERICA'S CRADLE TO PRISON PIPELINE: A REPORT OF THE CHILDREN'S DEFENSE FUND 1, 3–4 (2008).

267.   Omari Scott Simmons, *Lost in Transition: The Implications of Social Capital for Higher Education Access*, 97 NOTRE DAME L. REV. 205, 218–21 (2011) (highlighting the results of case studies from the Chicago and North Carolina public schools).

268.   Barack Obama, *What I Want for You—and Every Child in America*, PARADE, Jan. 18, 2009, at 4, available at: http://www.parade.com/news/2009/01/barack-obama-letter-to-my-daughters.html (last visited March 11, 2014).

269.   *See* Press Release, La. Fed'n of Teachers, Race to the Top: Frequently Asked Questions 1 (Mar. 4, 2010), available at: http://la.aft.org/files/article_assets/9AE1AFF5-BEB1-B947-B2FF905E66AE89D7.pdf (last visited March 11, 2014).

270.   ROD PAIGE & ELAINE WITTY, THE BLACK-WHITE ACHIEVEMENT GAP: WHY CLOSING IT IS THE GREATEST CIVIL RIGHTS ISSUE OF OUR TIME, 15 (2010) (internal citations omitted).

271.   20 U.S.C. § 6301 (2011). The Elementary and Secondary Education Act of 1965 was originally enacted April 11, 1965. It underwent a series of minor revisions from 1965 through 1978. The Act was extensively revised and restated by Act Nov. 1, 1978, P.L. 95-561. It was subsequently extensively revised and restated again in 1988, P.L. 100-297, 102 Stat. 130, and classified to 20 U.S.C. §§ 2701 et seq. It was extensively revised and restated again by Act Oct. 20, 1994, P.L. 103-382, 108 Stat. 3518, and classified to 20 U.S.C. §§ 6301 et seq. Finally, the Act underwent extensive amendments,

renumbering, reorganization of subject matter, and expansion of provisions by Act Jan. 8, 2002, P.L. 107-110 (also known as the No Child Left Behind Act of 2001).

272.   PL 107-110, codified as 20 U.S.C. §6301, *et seq.* On May 23, 2001, the House of Representatives favorably passed the bill by a vote of 384-45. Similarly, on June 14, 2001, the Senate passed it by a vote of 91-8. President Bush signed the new enactment into law on January 8, 2001. Indeed, NCLB was enacted as a bipartisan effort toward much needed education reform. Because NCLB was technically an amendment to Title I of the Education and Secondary Education Act of 1965, some education law scholars argue NCLB was a federal misapplication of Title I. *See, e.g.,* Derek W. Black, *The Congressional Failure to Enforce Equal Protection Through The Elementary and Secondary Education Act,* 90 B.U. L. REV. 313, 314 (2010). Specifically, Black argues that "[i]n particular, recent revisions of Title I, such as the No Child Left Behind Act, have been used to spur general school reform and political agendas more than to further non-discrimination and equity for poor students." *Id.* (internal citations omitted).

273.   Published scholarship has defined the concept of "school choice" for the purposes of education reform as follows: "Under school choice, parents have options that are restricted to public schools. For example, thirty-three states have open enrollment laws of varying degrees that allow students to attend public schools outside their home district, and eighteen states make open enrollment mandatory." John C. Goodman, *School Choice vs. School Choice,* 45 HOW. L. J. 375, 380 (2002) (citing Educ. Commission of the States, BUILDING ON PROGRESS: HOW READY ARE STATES TO IMPLEMENT PRESIDENT BUSH'S EDUCATION PLAN?, 14 (2001)) (hereinafter "Goodman").

274.   *See* Laurence Steinberg, BEYOND THE CLASSROOM: WHY SCHOOL REFORM HAS FAILED AND WHAT PARENTS NEED TO DO, 45-46 (Simon & Schuster Paperbacks 1996)(internal citations omitted).

275.   *Id.*

276.   *Id.* at 88-90 (discussing empirical data supporting the proposition that Asian students outperformed both white and Latino students, while African Americans achievement scores were the lowest of the four ethnic groups that were the subject of the case study.).

277.	*Id.* at 78.
278.	*Id.* at 83.
279.	PAIGE & WITTY, *supra* note 270, at 107.
280.	*Id.*
281.	Matthew Ladner & Matthew Brouillette, *The Impact of Charter Schools and Public School Choice on Public School Districts in Wayne County, Michigan*, 45 HOW. L.J. 395, 400-01 (internal citations omitted).
282.	Pub. L. No. 89-10, Declaration of Policy, Sec. 201, Elementary and Secondary Education Act of 1965.
283.	For the fiscal year 2010, Congress appropriated $14.5 billion to Title I, Part A of the Elementary and Secondary Education Act of 1965 (ESEA).
284.	US Dept. of Education, Office of the Undersecretary (2002), No Child Left Behind: A Desk Reference at http://www2.ed.gov/admins/lead/account/nclbreference/index.htm l?src=rt (hereinafter "Desktop Reference"), at p. 20. (last visited March 11, 2014).
285.	Title I is the funding mechanism of ESEA. The largest federal program funding elementary and secondary education, Congress allocates billions (more than $14billion in FY 2010) through Title I for additional instructional staff, professional development, extended-time programs, and other strategies for raising student achievement in high-poverty schools.
286.	Nick Lewin, *The No Child Left Behind Act of 2001: The Triumph of School Choice Over Racial Desegregation*, 12 GEO. J. POVERTY LAW & POL'Y 95, 101 (2005) (citing John F. Jennings, *Title I: Its Legislative History and Promise*, in TITLE I: COMPENSATORY EDUCATION AT THE CROSSROADS (Geoffrey D. Borman et al. eds. 2001)).
287.	Amy Reichbach, *The Power Behind the Promise: Enforcing No Child Left Behind to Improve Education*, 45 B.C.L. REV 667, 674 (2004). "Basic levels of achievement" are measured by the National Center for Education Statistics in the U.S. Department of Education. The National Assessment of Educational Progress (NEAP), commonly referred to as "the nation's report card," provides a continuing assessment of academic growth among America's schoolchildren. Officials began measuring growth using a national assessment in 1968.

Lamar Alexander and H. Thomas James, *The Nation's Report Card: Improving the Assessment of Student Achievement. Report of the Study Group; with a Review of the Report by a Committee of the National Academy of Education* (Cambridge, MA: National Academy of Education, 1987).

288.   See Pub. L. No. 100-418, OMNIBUS TRADE AND COMPETITIVENESS ACT OF 1988; TITLE VI -- EDUCATION AND TRAINING FOR AMERICAN COMPETITIVENESS

289.   Pub. L. No. 103-382. The Improving America's Schools Act followed the Goals 2000: Educate America Act (Pub. L. No. 103-227, repealed 2002), which allocated funds for states and communities that developed standards for students. *See* Chinh Q. Le, *Looking to the Future: Legal and Policy Options for Racially Integrated Education in the South and the Nation*, 88 N.C.L. REV 725 (2010).

290.   *Id.*

291.   Craig Livermore and Michael Lewchuck, *Centralized Standards and Decentralized Competition: Suggested Revisions for No Child Left Behind to Create Greater Educational Responsiveness Toward Disempowered Minority Groups*, 33 SETON HALL LEGIS. J. 433, 457 (2009).

292.   20 USCS § 6316 (a)(1)(A) (2011).

293.   20 USCS § 6316 (a)(1)(C) (2011) and 20 USCS § 6316 (a)(2) (2011).

294.   20 USCS § 6321 (b).

295.   20 USCS § 6319 (a)(1) (2011).

296.   20 USCS § 6301 (9) (2011). *See also* 20 USCS § 6368, which requires "scientifically based reading research" for professional development and assessment.

297.   20 USCS § 6301 (10) (2011).

298.   20 USCS § 6301 (9) (2011).

299.   LA. REV. STAT. § 17:10.5 (A)(1) (emphasis added).

300.   Under Louisiana law, there are five types of charter schools. *See, generally,* LA. REV. STAT. § 17:3973. Specifically, Type 1 charters are new, start-up schools, chartered with the local school board; Type 2 charters are either new start-up or conversions, authorized by BESE; Type 3 are conversions chartered with the local school board; Type 4 are new start-up or conversion schools, chartered with BESE; and Type 5 are preexisting schools transferred to the RSD.

301.   *See, generally,* LA. REV. STAT. §§ 10.6 & 10.7. In 1989, New Jersey became the first state to take over a local school district. That year alone, Kentucky, New Mexico, South Carolina, Texas and West Virginia also enacted district takeover laws. Joseph O. Oluwole & Preston C. Greene, III, *State Takeovers of School Districts: Race and the Equal Protection Clause,* 42 IND. L. REV. 343, 343 (2009) (internal citations omitted). By 2004, twenty-nine different states had followed suit. *Id.*

302.   Danielle Holley-Walker, *The Accountability Cycle: The recovery School District Act and New Orleans' Charter Schools,* 40 Conn. L. Rev. 125, 135-36 (2007) (internal citations omitted).

303.   *See* UNITED STATES COMMISSION ON CIVIL RIGHTS, BECOMING LESS SEPARATE?: SCHOOL DESEGREGATION, JUSTICE DEPARTMENT ENFORCEMENT AND THE PURSUIT OF UNITARY STATUS, 141-45 (2007) (hereinafter "CIVIL RIGHTS").

304.   *See, e.g.,* Derrick A. Bell, Jr., *Serving Two Masters: Integration Ideals and Client Interests in School Desegregation Litigation,* in CRITICAL RACE THEORY: THE KEY WRITINGS THAT FORMED THE MOVEMENT, 8 (New Press 1995) (Kimberlé Crenshaw, ed.) (discussing the foregoing as a perspective held by many advocates in the civil rights community); *see also* Kristi L. Bowman, *A New Strategy for Pursuing Racial and Ethnic Equality in Public Schools,* 1 DUKE F. FOR L. & SOC. CHANGE 47, 52 (2009) (internal citations omitted) (hereinafter "Bowman").

305.   *See, e.g., Swann v. Charlotte-Mecklenburg Board of Education,* 402 U.S. 1 (1971) (authoring the use of busing); *San Antonio Independent School District v. Rodriguez,* 411 U.S. 1 (1973) (holding that inequalities in school funding do not deny equal protection); *see also, Milliken v. Bradley II,* 433 U.S. 267 (1977) (holding that courts may order states to pay for compensatory and remedial programs for school children who have been subjected to segregation).

306.   *See, Acts 9.*

307.   *See, e.g., Luke 4:14-20.*